GRADES K-2

Smart Strands™

Content Options For:

- ◆ **NUMBER**
- ◆ **GEOMETRY**
- ◆ **MEASUREMENT**
- ◆ **ALGEBRA**
- ◆ **DATA**

NUMBER • GEOMETRY • MEASUREMENT • ALGEBRA • DATA • NUMBER • GEOMETRY • MEASUREMENT • ALGEBRA • GEOMETRY • NUMBER • MEASUREMENT • ALGEBRA • DATA • NUMBER • GEOMETRY • MEASUREMENT • ALGEBRA • DATA • NUMBER • GEOMETRY • M

◆ **Creative Publications®**

Writers
Dan Brutlag, Tim Erickson, Anne Goodrow,
Mark Gordon, Nancy Homan, Rhea Irvine,
Elizabeth Javor, Sarkis Kel-Artinian, Marie Lagos,
Scott Lape, Taryn LaRaja, Heather McDonald,
Christina Myren, Margo Nanny, Gene Novak,
Kathryn Walker

Project Editors
Amy Cohen, Cynthia Reak, Kelly Stewart,
Sharon Wheeler

Editors
Sarah LeForge, Ann Roper, Glenda Stewart

Art Director
Violeta Diaz

Designers
Amy Feldman, Meg Saint-Loubert

Illustrators
Chrystal Baudot, Amy Feldman, Mamiko Sakurai,
Sharon Spurlock

Production Director
Edward Lazar

Production Coordinator
Joe Shines

Manufacturing Coordinator
Michelle Berardinelli

Production
Morgan-Cain & Associates

©1999 Creative Publications
Two Prudential Plaza, Suite 1175
Chicago, IL 60601
Printed in the United States of America
ISBN 0-7622-1159-8
 2 3 4 5 6 7 8 9 10. 03 02 01 00 99

Contents

Introduction to Smart Strands

What is Smart Strands?

Smart Strands is a collection of lessons and week-long investigations designed to provide you with flexible options for teaching your mathematics curriculum. Each of the three books in the Smart Strands series spans multi-grade levels and contains lessons in the following content areas: Number, Geometry, Measurement, Algebra, and Data.

How do I use Smart Strands?

You have several options for integrating Smart Strands into your regular mathematics program. You can select lessons to replace your current curriculum or to supplement a particular concept. Smart Strands lessons allow you to delve in greater depth into a topic your students find particularly interesting, or to select lessons that fulfill the curriculum needs of your district or state guidelines. Because each Smart Strands book spans grade levels, you have the flexibility of selecting lessons that provide students with review as well as challenge opportunities.

If you have MathLand, you will need to make choices in deciding what and when to teach a particular lesson or lessons. Compare the Key Mathematical Ideas in the Guidebook with those in Smart Strands to determine how Smart Strands lessons align with Guidebook investigations and how you might integrate one with the other. One option is to substitute Guidebook investigations with lessons from Smart Strands. Another option is to spend less time on the Guidebook investigation and interweave the Smart Strands and Guidebook content. For example, you might choose to add Day Trips about symmetry flips, turns, and transformations to your geometry week, extending the Guidebook week by a day or two, or you might decide to teach the data lessons from Smart Strands rather than the data unit from the Guidebook.

If you teach in a multi-grade setting or have students spanning a range of levels, you will find the grade-level spans of Smart Strands particularly helpful in meeting the needs of your students. Look at different grade-level editions of Smart Strands for content that would also be appropriate for your students.

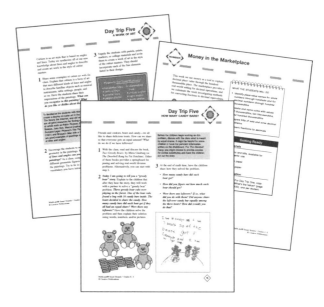

How is Smart Strands organized?

Each Smart Strands book contains 15 weeks of instruction. Some lessons are intended as week-long investigations that develop students' understanding as the week progresses. These weeks have a Setting Out (Monday), Along the Way (Tuesday, Wednesday, and Thursday), and Looking Back (Friday). Another type of Smart Strands week is a collection of Day Trips, which are designed for flexibility. Depending on the concepts you wish to have your students explore, you might choose to teach anywhere from one to five Day Trip lessons some weeks.

What should I look for in Smart Strands lessons?

The Introduction page that opens each week's lesson contains important information to help you plan your week.

Key Mathematical Ideas highlights the math concepts students will explore during the week.

Prior Knowledge provides important guidelines for the skills and experiences your students should have before working on the week's lessons.

What the Students Will Do outlines the activities students will be engaged in during the upcoming week.

Getting Ready informs you about any supplies you will need for the week's lessons and materials to prepare prior to beginning each lesson.

Numbered Steps guide you through each lesson; suggestions for discussion questions and instructions to students are highlighted in bold italic print.

Shaded Boxes, or mentor statements, give advice, tips, and background information to support your teaching and help you facilitate an investigation.

Discussion Questions encourage students to think and to talk about their solution strategies. By asking students to respond to questions, you help them to clarify their ideas and thought processes.

Student Work samples show possible approaches to problems presented in the activity. Your students' work may look similar—or quite different!

Interview Assessment questions allow you to check students' understanding as they work and to make instructional choices based on students' needs.

Home Work suggestions support the learning students are doing on a particular day or for the week.

Math Journal prompts allow students opportunities to reflect on their learning and provide you with another window to their thinking and level of understanding.

Side Trips are options you can use with the whole class, pairs, or individual students to enrich, extend, or review the week's investigation.

Ongoing Projects are intended to be continued or repeated throughout the year.

Puzzling Farm Problems

This week we begin an exploration of open-ended problems that the children may solve using a variety of child-generated strategies. The problems have many ways to arrive at one solution or have multiple solutions (as in the legs problems). Each problem is complex and may ask the children to use more than one operation to solve it. Each problem also requires at least one class period to complete. The children compare, find unknown parts, work with part-part-whole, use groupings of ten, and measure using nonstandard units.

Key Mathematical Ideas

★ There may be more than one way to solve a mathematical problem.

★ Some mathematical problems may have more than one solution.

★ A relationship exists between the size of a unit and the number of units needed in a measurement.

Prior Knowledge

Some experience using groups of ten is helpful. You may want to discuss what children know about farm life.

WHAT THE CHILDREN WILL DO

- Solve story problems using a variety of child-generated strategies
- Find solutions using manipulatives
- Explain solutions using numbers, words, and pictures

Getting Ready

Materials

- Rainbow Tiles, beans, or other counting materials, 100 per group

- LinkerCubes, 100 per pair

- full sheets of paper for each child

- chart paper

- sticky notes

- toothpicks, 50 per pair

Preparation

 • Provide children's literature about farms and farm animals. An optional book for Days Two and Three is *Legs* written by Mike Artell. For Day Trip Three, you may want to prepare cover sheets for the class book.

A farmer has many jobs. What happens if she gets tired? Today we solve a two-step problem to determine if Farmer Jane remembered to feed all her animals.

1 Tell the class the following Forgetful Farmer story. *On Farmer Jane's farm there were 2 ducks, 3 pigs, 4 chickens, 5 cows, and 6 horses. One evening she was very tired. She fed 14 animals and then went back to the farmhouse to sleep. When she woke early the next morning, she wondered if she remembered to feed all the animals. Did she feed all the animals?*

2 After discussing the problem, give each child a full sheet of paper for recording. *You may use any materials in the room to help you find the answer. Draw and tell about how you would show Farmer Jane whether she fed all her animals. Be sure to tell what you did to find your solution.*

3 As the children work, encourage them to tell you about their ideas. Record this additional information on sticky notes and attach it later to their work. If children have trouble writing about their solutions, have them dictate their ideas to you or another adult.

Did Farmer Jane remember to feed all the animals?

Mikiko No. She had 20 animals to feed.

How do you know?

Mikiko I added; 2 and 3 is 5, 5 plus 5 is 10. Four and 6 is 10, and 10 plus 10 makes 20.

She fed 14 animals, so how many did she forget to feed?

---

4 When most of the class has completed this task, have four or five children share their solution strategies.

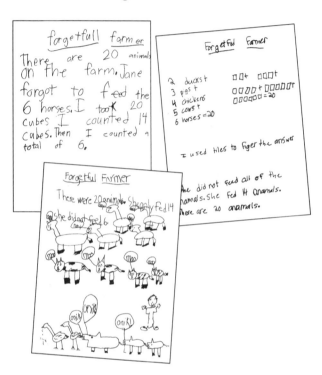

Expect a variety of responses. Some children may have complete, well-explained answers that include the number sentence 20 − 14 = 6. Others may only be able to state that Farmer Jane had 20 animals, unaware of how many were not fed. After the children have a chance to see successful solutions, you may want to allow time for some of the children to revise their answers.

Feel free to change the numbers in the problem to fit your children. For example, an easier version of this problem might be: Farmer Jane had 2 ducks, 3 pigs, and 4 chickens. One evening she fed 7 animals and then went back to the farmhouse to sleep.

Today's challenge is to find the number of animal legs in Farmer Jane's barn. How many legs on a duck? a spider? a cow?

1 *What kinds of animals might Farmer Jane have in her barn?* As the children suggest animals, list them on chart paper.

2 *How many legs are there on each of these animals?* Add the number of legs for each animal to the chart as the children respond to this question.

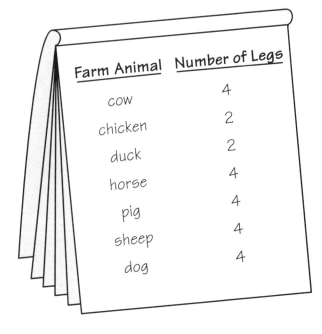

Farm Animal	Number of Legs
cow	4
chicken	2
duck	2
horse	4
pig	4
sheep	4
dog	4

3 *One day Farmer Jane walked into her barn and saw two chickens, one cow, and one horse. How many legs did she see?* List each animal's name and number of legs on the chalkboard. Give each child a blank sheet of paper to respond to this question. *Draw and tell how you found the answer to this problem.*

Be ready to take notes or dictation from children who have emerging reading and writing skills. With some children, only a partial understanding may be depicted by their written work. If this is the case, you or another adult might ask the child, **Tell me about your answer.** Add a note about the response to the back of the child's work.

4 As children finish, have them share their answers in pairs.

- *How many legs are there?*

- *How do you know?*

- *Did someone find the answer a different way? How?*

5 After several pairs have shared their solutions, collect the papers and save them for the next lesson.

The book *Legs* written by Mike Artell, can provide a springboard for this problem and the next. *Legs* is a lift-the-flap book written in rhyme. It features a variety of four-legged, six-legged, and eight-legged creatures, each concealed behind a flap. Children guess what—or who—is behind each flap. While the book is not necessary to introduce these two lessons, it can become a spark for the discussion.

Children are given the number of legs, but not the names of the animals. What possible animals might be represented?

1 Have four or five children share their work from yesterday. Choose samples of work that show different ways of representing the answer. Then review the chart of animal names and number of legs from the previous lesson. The children may want to add additional animals.

2 Discuss with the class possible solutions to the following problem. *Farmer Jane walked into her barn. She saw eight legs behind one of the stalls. What animals might belong to those eight legs?*

Laura	It could be 2 horses; 4 legs and 4 legs make 8 legs.
Awenita	Or maybe 2 chickens and 1 pig; 2 plus 2 plus 4 makes 8 legs.

3 Change the problem for the children to solve individually or in pairs. *Behind another stall in her barn, Farmer Jane saw 14 legs. What animals might be behind that stall?*

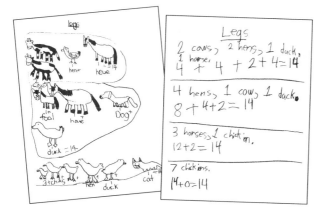

4 At the end of math time, have the children share their solutions. After each child has shared, ask, *Does anyone have a different solution?* See how many different solutions your class generated.

5 Bind the solutions into a class book titled *Fourteen Legs.*

The numbers in this problem can be changed to make the problems easier or more difficult. You may want to challenge some of the children to find and depict more than one solution to this problem. Kindergarten children can use small plastic farm animals to count the actual legs as they are trying to make a total of 14.

Home Work

For homework this week have the children write Puzzling Farm problems of their own, including solutions. Children can have a family member try to solve their problems.

Today we work with tens to find the solution to a problem. Each horse eats ten bales of hay a month. How many bales of hay does Farmer Jane need to order?

1 *What is a bale of hay?* Explain how hay is bundled into bales to make it easier to store.

2 *Farmer Jane has seven horses. Each horse eats about ten bales of hay a month. At the end of this month, Farmer Jane had two bales of hay left. How many bales does she need to buy for the next month?* Discuss the problem with the class.

3 Give each child a full sheet of blank paper. *Today you are going to draw and tell about the number of bales that Farmer Jane needs to order. Be sure to explain how you got your answer.*

4 End math time by getting together to discuss the day's work. Have the children focus on the various strategies they used to solve the problem.

How many bales of hay does Farmer Jane need?	
Laura	I counted by tens to 70. Then I counted backward to 68.
Kalil	My answer is 70. She might need two extra bales if the horses eat more.

 Math Journal   Children might like to invent their own How Many Bales? problems. In their journals they can show their solutions.

Children explore the relationship of two different items used to measure length.

1 *The farmer has two sons—Jake and Devin. Jake measured Devin two ways. First he measured Devin using toothpicks, and then he measured him using LinkerCubes. Devin was 29 toothpicks long. With the LinkerCubes he was 68 cubes long. Why were the numbers different?* Discuss this question with the class. (You might choose to use unsharpened pencils with younger children.)

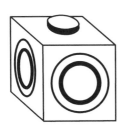

2 *Work with a partner to measure each other. First measure from head to toe using toothpicks. Then use LinkerCubes to take the same measurement. Keep track of the numbers for each. Measure both of you.* Give each child a piece of blank paper. *Draw and tell* (write) *about the results of measuring each other.*

Observe the children as they measure. Do they start at the same place each time? Do the children place the items end to end or leave a gap between each? Are they able to use one-to-one correspondence to count the items correctly? Do they use some sort of grouping (twos, fives, or tens) to help them count more efficiently?

3 When most of the children have finished, gather the children together to share their ideas about why the measurements were different. *Did you get different numbers? Why do you think that happened?*

This is a puzzling problem for some children. Older children might be able to reach a generalization that the longer the item used to measure, the fewer of this measure are needed. Or they might say that if you use LinkerCubes, you need more LinkerCubes to measure the same distance. This understanding develops over time. Not every child in your class will be able to express this.

Interview Assessment

Approach pairs as they work, and ask, *Did you get the same number when you measured with toothpicks and with LinkerCubes?*

How Many? How Much?

How Many? is a question we ask this week as we explore strategies for multiplication and division problems that the children may solve using a variety of child-generated solutions. Each problem is complex and may require more than one step to solve.

Key Mathematical Ideas

★ There may be more than one way to solve a mathematical problem.

★ Multiplication may be represented by repeated addition, arrays, and/or area models.

★ The unknown in division may be the number of groups or the number of elements in each group.

Prior Knowledge

Children need to know about joining and separating sets. Experience using groups of ten is helpful.

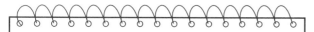

WHAT THE CHILDREN WILL DO

• Devise a variety of strategies for multiplication

• Solve division problems in which the unknown is the number of elements in each group

• Solve division problems in which the unknown is the number of groups

Getting Ready

Materials

• LinkerCubes, 100 at each table

• Rainbow Tiles, 100 at each table

• full sheets of paper

• chart paper

• Overhead Rainbow Tiles or LinkerCubes, 8 each of 2 different colors

Preparation

• For Day Trip Two, make a "watch chart," and a watch cut-out worksheet (optional, see page 12). For Day Trip Three, make a transparency of 1-inch grid paper, (page 106). Optional for Day Trip Five, locate the books *Two Greedy Bears* by Mirra Ginsburg, published by Macmillan in 1976, or *The Doorbell Rang* by Pat Hutchins, published by Greenwillow in 1986.

Suppose for a science project, each child in our class plants beans. How many beans will we plant if each person plants 2 beans? If each person plants 3 beans?

1 *Have you ever planted seeds?* Have the children share their experiences planting and growing seeds. *If everyone in our class planted 2 beans for a science experiment, how many seeds would we plant all together?* As a class, formulate a plan for solving the problem. *How can we find out? What could we do first?* Work the problem as a class, making cubes or tiles available for children's use.

2 Explain to the children that now they will work with a partner to solve a similar problem. *Everyone in Mrs. Myren's class planted 3 lima beans. She has 27 children in her class. How many beans did they plant all together? You may use anything in the room that might help you figure out the answer. Use numbers, words, and/or pictures to show how you solved the problem.*

Children often solve this problem in interesting ways. They may use repeated addition, area models, or arrays. One pair of children repeatedly took 3 LinkerCubes and made 27 piles. Another group put 3 beans on each of 27 desks, then gathered them and counted the beans. Observe the children and make notes as they work. If appropriate, change the difficulty of the numbers in the problem to suit your class.

3 At the end of math time, have the children share the strategies they used to solve the problem.

- *How many beans did Mrs. Myren's class plant?*

- *Did anyone have a different answer?*

- *How did you figure it out? Did you think the answer would be greater? less? Or did it seem like the right amount of beans for 27 children?*

- *Did someone solve the problem a different way? How?*

Day Trip Two
HOW MANY WAYS CAN MARIA ARRANGE HER WATCH?

Some watches come with interchangeable bands and rings around the face allowing us to create many different watches. Our question for today challenges us to figure out just how many different "looks" are possible.

1 On chart paper, draw a simple watch. Make the watchband blue and draw a red circle around the face of the watch. Then show a black, green, and brown watchband. Also draw another yellow circle that would fit around the face.

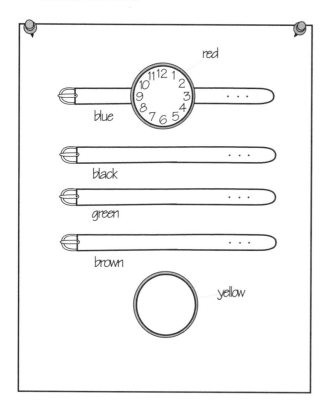

2 *Maria has 4 colors of bands: blue, black, green, and brown. The watch has two rings that go around the clock part: red and yellow. She can change her watch. What is one way Maria could change her watch so it looks different? How many different ways can Maria's watch look?*

3 Have the children work together in pairs. *Think of all the different ways that Maria's watch could look. Then draw a picture that shows all the ways you found. Tell how you know you found all the different ways Maria can change her watch.*

4 At the end of class, have pairs share how they solved the problem. *How many different watches did you make? How did you organize your work so that you knew the watches were all different?*

For kindergarten children, you may want to make a simple worksheet that has four watchbands and two rings to color and cut out. A possible worksheet is shown.

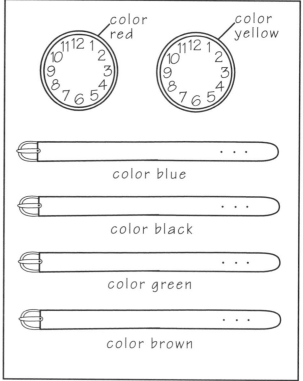

MathLand® Smart Strands • Grades K–2
© Creative Publications

Today we become designers. How many tiles will it take to cover the P.E. equipment room floor?

1 As a class, discuss different types of flooring, including a tile floor. *Today we are going to use Rainbow Tiles to build a model of a tile floor. First, we'll build a model floor that is 2 tiles wide and 3 tiles long.* Use transparent Rainbow Tiles or LinkerCubes to build a floor model on the overhead projector. *How many tiles does it take to cover this floor? How did you figure it out?*

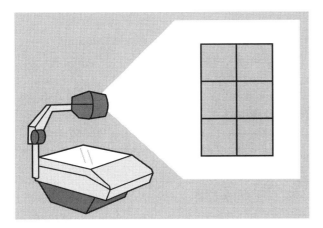

2 *What if we wanted to make a floor that is 3 tiles wide and 4 tiles long? What would it look like? How many tiles would it take? Use the tiles at your table to build that floor.*

3 *How could you use graph paper to record your floor so other people would know what your floor looks like?* As the children share their ideas, demonstrate on the overhead projector, using a transparency of 1-inch grid paper and overhead Rainbow Tiles.

4 *Today you and your partner are going to figure out how many tiles we would need to cover the floor of the P. E. equipment room. The floor is 4 tiles wide and 8 tiles long. Build the floor. Then trace around the tiles on the grid paper.* Have the children write a note to the principal telling her how many tiles to order from the tile company.

5 End math time by having the children share their work and solutions with the class.

As children share their work, you may hear varied solution strategies. Some children will find the total using one-to-one counting or repeated addition (8 + 8 + 8 + 8 = 32). Other children may use a derived fact strategy (8 + 8 = 16 and 16 + 16 = 32). Discussing their solution strategies provides opportunities for children to learn new approaches to solving problems from each other.

Home Work

For homework, give each child a sheet of 1-inch grid paper. Have the children design a tile floor that is 6 tiles long by 4 tiles wide. *What does the floor look like? How many tiles does it take to make?*

Our class is making math journals. There seems to be enough paper for everyone, but how can we know for sure?

1 Hold up 60 sheets of blank paper. *Ms. Takenada's class decided to make math journals. They wanted to put 4 pieces of paper in each journal. How many journals can they make from 60 pieces of paper? Will there be enough journals for all 27 children in the class?* Write the important numbers on the chalkboard as a reference for the children as they work.

> One journal = 4 pieces of paper
> How many journals can the class make with 60 pieces of paper?
> 27 children in the class
> Is there enough paper?

2 *Work with your partner to figure out how many journals Ms. Takenada's class can make from the paper.* Give each pair a blank piece of paper to record their thinking. Have LinkerCubes or Rainbow Tiles accessible for children to use as counters. Before children begin to work, you might want to make a sample journal as a class and discuss ideas for getting started on the problem.

> **How do you plan to work on this problem?**
>
> Amy I'm going to put 4 cubes in each pile and see how many piles I have.
>
> Luis I think we can make 12 journals. I'll count out 12 four times and see if there's any left.
>
> **Will 12 journals be enough for all the children?**
>
> Luis No, they need 27 journals and 27 is more than 12.

3 After the pairs have had time to solve the problem and record their solution, have the children share the strategies they used.

- *How did you and your partner work on this problem?*

- *Is there enough paper for every child to have a journal? How do you know?*

- *Did anyone solve the problem a different way? What did you do?*

4 For children who finish early and realize that there are not enough journals, extend the problem. Ask them to tell how many more journals are needed. *How many more sheets of paper does the class need?*

Interview Assessment

During the week, observe children's problem-solving strategies. Do pairs discuss a plan before getting started? Do they work cooperatively? Do they try different strategies? Are they able to articulate their ideas?

Friends and cookies, bears and candy—we all like to share delicious treats. How can we share so that everyone gets an equal amount? What do we do if we have leftovers?

1 With the class, read and discuss the book, *Two Greedy Bears,* by Mirra Ginsburg (or *The Doorbell Rang* by Pat Hutchins). Either of these books provides a springboard for posing and solving real-world division problems. Alternatively, you can start with step 2.

2 *Today I am going to tell you a "greedy bear" story.* Explain to the children that after they hear the story, they will work with a partner to solve a "greedy bear" problem. *Three greedy bear cubs were playing in the forest. One of the bear cubs found a bag with 16 candy bars inside. The bears decided to share the candy. How many candy bars did each bear get if they all had an equal share? Were there any leftovers?* Have the children solve the problem and then explain their solution using words, numbers, and/or pictures.

Before the children begin working on this problem, discuss with the class what is meant by equal shares. It might be helpful for some children to have the pertinent information written on the chalkboard. For *The Doorbell Rang,* you might choose to provide cookies (or cookie substitutes) and have the children act out the story.

3 At the end of math time, have the children share how they solved the problem.

- *How many candy bars did each bear get?*

- *How did you figure out how much each bear should get?*

- *Were there any leftovers? If so, what did you do with them? Did anyone share the left-over candy bar equally among the three bears? How did (could) you do that?*

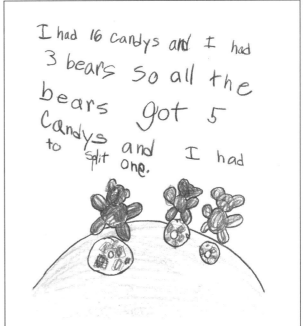

Between 10 and 20

This week we create real-world addition and subtraction problems for our classmates to solve. The stories give us practice with number combinations for numbers to 20. We develop our own ways to use manipulatives, modeling, counting strategies, and derived facts to solve problems. Creating equations that correspond to our stories helps us understand that equations are a meaningful way to write about what has happened. Throughout this week, we have many opportunities to think about and apply the relationship between addition and subtraction.

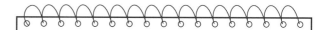

WHAT THE CHILDREN WILL DO

- Write modeled and original story problems involving basic facts to 20
- Solve addition and subtraction problems using reasoning-based methods
- Discuss solutions with classmates
- Make class books of problems

Key Mathematical Ideas

★ There are a number of different ways to solve problems involving addition and subtraction.

★ Equations are one way to represent a story situation.

★ Strong part-part-whole understanding helps us construct the relationship between addition and subtraction.

★ Patterns in related addition and subtraction sentences can be used to solve problems.

Getting Ready

Materials

- LinkerCubes

- chart paper

- full sheets of paper

- 9" × 12" construction paper, enough for several class books

- stapler

Prior Knowledge

Children should have a strong foundation in number relationships for numbers 1 through 10, as well as experience writing complete equations to tell about addition and subtraction situations.

We begin this week with story problems involving the numbers just beyond 10. The problems get us started looking at number pairs for the numbers between 10 and 20.

1 *Here's a Start and Finish story. I'll start it. You finish it.* Write the story on chart paper as you tell it. ***Sam needed 16 cookies. He bought 2 kinds of cookies. Nine were chocolate-chip cookies and....*** Have a child finish the story. ***What equation could we write to tell about this situation?*** Children may suggest both the addition equation $9 + 7 = 16$ and the subtraction equation $16 - 9 = 7$. Both can be valid expressions of the way a child has thought about the problem situation. Have children explain why they think their equation fits the story.

Young children often think about subtraction situations in terms of addition (9 and what makes 16?) rather than "take away." Children who use this approach—figuring out the missing part—are demonstrating their strong part-part-whole understanding. Be sure to support this thinking, in which children use the relationship of addition to subtraction, and note when individuals use it to solve problems.

2 *Let's write Start and Finish stories for numbers between 10 and 20. You will start a story, exchange papers with a partner, and then write the finish of your partner's story. Return the story to your partner. When you get your own story back, check to see that the finish is a correct ending. Then write an equation for your story at the bottom of the page.*

3 When pairs have finished writing their stories, bring the children together to discuss their stories and equations.

- *How did you figure out the number to finish the story?*
- *Does this equation tell about the story? Why?*
- *Does anyone have a story that uses the same three numbers in a different way?*

Notice that children use fact-family reasoning on their own to finish the stories. Often they add up to solve subtraction problems or use their thinking about parts of numbers flexibly. Children may be using a larger set of related facts as well, especially as they use their knowledge of the doubles and near-doubles strategies.

4 Some children may be interested in exploring the idea that the addends in a problem can appear in any order without changing the result. Let them discuss this idea with each other. They may point out examples on the chalkboard. Suggest modeling with counters to prove that this idea is valid. You might suggest that children act out buying two toys at the store. *Does the order in which you buy the toys change how much you spend? What if you were buying three things?*

During the next several days, we'll write some new types of story problems and bind them into class books for our library. As we work, we'll gain more experience with number pairs for the numbers 11 through 19.

1 Each day tell one or more of the stories presented here. Record each story on chart paper as you tell it. Then have children write their own stories based on the model. Children may refer to the models while writing their own stories during the next three days.

2 *Let's continue to explore the numbers between 10 and 20. I'm going to tell a few Between 10 and 20 stories. Then it will be your turn to write stories for the class to solve.* Begin by telling the Two Pockets story.

3 Have children finish the story. *Write an equation that tells about the story on the back of your paper.* Then have the children write their own stories using the stories you tell as a model.

4 When children are ready, have them bring their stories to a reading circle. Have LinkerCubes, pencils, and paper available for children to use as they solve each other's stories. *Who has a story problem for us to solve?* When a story has been shared and children have had a chance to solve it, call on volunteers to explain how they solved it and tell their answers.

Two Pockets

Miranda had two pockets. She knew she had 16 cents in her pockets, but she couldn't remember how much money she had in each pocket. Miranda reached into one pocket and pulled out 7 cents. Then she knew she had _____ cents in her other pocket.

5 Remember to allow time each day for children to share their stories and discuss their solution strategies. You may choose to vary the discussion format. At times have children report on their own stories, explaining their solution strategies. Alternatively, have children present their stories, then ask the whole class to solve the problem.

Home Work

For homework this week, have children write an original addition or subtraction problem based on their family, home, or neighborhood. The story should involve a number between 10 and 20.

MathLand® Smart Strands • Grades K–2
© Creative Publications

Snack Stand

A group of children were lined up at a snack stand. There were 8 children in line for popcorn. The rest were in line for nachos. Sam knew that if he got in line for popcorn there would be the same number of children in each line. How many children were lined up for nachos?

The Snack Stand problem may be difficult for children to understand. When you introduce the problem, see if any children propose acting it out, then follow their lead. As children solve the problems they write, allow plenty of time for them to model their other strategies: using cubes, drawings, or counting. In creating problems like this one, children will be getting practice with the doubles facts, from which many related facts for the numbers 11 through 20 can be obtained.

Interview Assessment

As children write their story problems, say, *Tell me about the story you're creating. What number completes the story? How did you figure that out?*

Up the Stairs

Luis was going up the stairs to his classroom. There were 12 stairs to climb, and he was on the fifth stair. He knew he had ____ stairs to go.

6 At the end of each day, collect the children's stories. On the last day, have children who have finished writing help you staple several stories together with covers. Select a mix of problems for each book. Let children title the covers, *Our Between 10 and 20 Stories*. Partners may read finished books together. Keep the books in the class library. Invite children to take the books home to share as well.

Today we write a story to describe an equation we are given. What other stories can we write using the same set of numbers?

1 At the chalkboard, write the equation $10 - 7 = 3$. ***Who can make up a story that tells about this equation?*** Call on one child to share a story. Then ask, ***Who can use these same numbers—3, 7, and 10— to tell a different story? What equation can you write to tell that story?*** Call on one child to share a story and to write an equation that tells about it on the chalkboard. ***Tell us why you think this equation goes with your story.***

2 ***Who thought of an addition or subtraction story that has a different equation?*** Have children share the stories they created for equations (using 3, 7, and 10) not yet recorded on the board. Each speaker should write the new equation on the board. Remember that children may use thinking about addition to solve a subtraction situation, and equations may reflect that fact.

3 If no child has created a story for one of the possible equations in this fact family, offer a story yourself. Then ask the children what equation they would write for the story.

4 When the four fact-family equations have been written on the board, ask, ***Can anyone write a different equation with these numbers?*** Explore with the class the ideas children share. ***Are you convinced these are all the possible equations?***

What different equations can you write using 7, 3, and 10?

Michael   There are only two equations for adding 7 and 3—either 3 plus 7 or 7 plus 3 make 10.

Celia   For subtraction, you can take 3 or 7 away from 10. That's all you can do.

There were 3 strawberries. 7 more got picked.
There are 10 strawberries now.

$3 + 7 = 10$

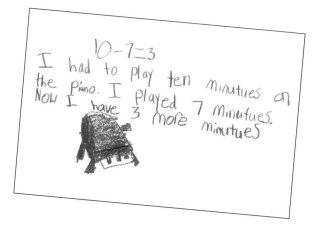

$10 - 7 = 3$
I had to play ten minutues on
the Piano. I played 7 minutues.
Now I have 3 more minutues

5 Discuss the term *fact family* with the class. *Sometimes groups of equations like these are called* **fact families.** *Why do you think that is?* Let children share their ideas about how the equations are related.

6 *Let's write fact-family stories. Choose a number between 10 and 20. Create a story for each fact-family equation of your number.* Tell the children to write each story on a separate page.

7 When children have finished writing their stories say, *Write the equations for your stories, in order, on a separate page. This will be the last page in your book.* This last page will give readers the opportunity to solve the problems themselves.

8 Have children make covers for their books. Each book should include a page at the beginning for readers to sign their names. Finished books can be placed in the class library as well as be taken home for family members to read and sign. Some children may need extra time to finish their stories and books.

Side Trip

Stories and More Stories

Three ways to extend children's experiences with story problems are described below.

- Have children share their original story problems with the class. The class should discuss whether a story is like any of those they wrote this week.

- Have children compose problems similar to an original problem that has already been shared.

- Place materials for writing and binding story problem books at a center. Children may make individual books using several pages to write and illustrate one story problem, or they may want to bind a collection of several problems into one book.

How Many Equal Parts?

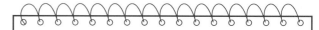

Equal-size parts are what we look for this week as we explore strategies for identifying parts of a whole. We use our intuitive ways of thinking to solve problems involving common fractions. The special ways we learn to talk about fractions and write about them help us communicate about parts of a whole.

Key Mathematical Ideas

★ When a whole object is broken into equal parts, each part is a fraction of the whole.

★ Special language and terms are helpful for describing and naming the equal parts of a whole.

★ Fractions can be represented symbolically.

★ There may be more than one way to name fractional parts of a set.

Prior Knowledge

Children will bring to this work their informal experiences with shapes and with situations that call for fair shares. Several of these experiences can serve as introductions to fractions. For Day Trips Four and Five, children should have had experiences dividing shapes such as circles and rectangles into equal parts.

WHAT THE CHILDREN WILL DO

- Solve problems involving common fractions
- Find fractional parts of a whole
- Describe parts of a whole
- Name fractional parts
- Represent fractions symbolically

Getting Ready

Materials

- LinkerCubes, at least 100 in each of three colors

- 12" × 18" construction paper, 1 sheet per pair

- 9" × 12" construction paper, 1 sheet per child

- Half sheets of paper

- Chart paper

Preparation

 • For Day Trip One, cut 4" × 4" squares, and 3" × 5" rectangles, 5 of each per pair. Optional—find the book *Eating Fractions* by Bruce Macmillan (Scholastic, 1991). For Day Trip Two, cut yarn into 24" lengths, 4 pieces per pair. Optional—find the book *We Can Share It* by Sarah Tatler (Scott Foresman, 1993).

Have you ever shared a sandwich with someone? Did each person get an equal part? Today we find many ways to make halves of something. Are all halves alike?

1 *Tina and Tico are sharing a sandwich. Tico says, "I can cut the sandwich here and we will both have fair shares." Tina says, "But I know another way I can cut the sandwich and we can still have fair shares." Is there more than one way to cut a sandwich into two equal parts?*

2 Tell the children that they are going to pretend to share a sandwich with a friend. *See if you can find more than two ways to divide a sandwich into halves.* Distribute several squares of paper to each pair. *You may fold, draw on, and cut the papers.*

3 When children are ready, have them make recordings that show and tell about the ways they found to make halves. They may draw the shapes or paste them on construction paper.

The book *Eating Fractions* by Bruce Macmillan is an excellent starting point for discussing fractional parts. Two children make lunch together and share fractional parts of a number of foods. The book shows halves, thirds, and fourths, and how to represent fractions symbolically.

4 When the recordings are finished, bring the children together to discuss their results. *How do you know those parts are halves?* Children may fold the paper or cut it into parts and place the parts on top of each other to see that the parts are congruent.

5 *Suppose sandwich bread had a rectangular shape. With your partners, try dividing rectangles into halves.* Distribute paper rectangles. *Make a record that shows and tells what you find out.*

6 When the children are ready, bring them together and discuss their results. Then ask, *If you cut a circular pizza in half, would the half look like any of the shapes you've found today? Is half of a big pizza the same size as half of a little pizza?* The discussion should bring out the idea that the size and shape of a half are related to the size and shape of the object being shared.

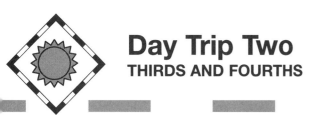

Day Trip Two
THIRDS AND FOURTHS

Today we solve problems involving equal parts of a field and equal parts of a rope. Which is larger, $\frac{1}{2}$, $\frac{1}{3}$, or $\frac{1}{4}$?

1 *Farmer Jane has two fields of the same size and shape. In one field, she wants to make equal-size pens for 3 animals. In the other, she wants to make equal-size pens for 4 animals.* Distribute 2 half sheets of paper to pairs. *Show a way to divide one paper into 3 equal-size pens. Then show a way to make 4 equal-size pens on the other paper.* (Some possible ways are shown below.)

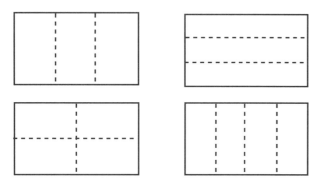

2 When the children are ready, have them share their solutions. *How do you know the pens are equal parts of the field? Are there different ways to make 3 or 4 equal parts? What do we call 1 out of 3 equal parts?* Children may suggest "a third" or "one third." *What do we call 1 out of 4 equal parts? Which has more room, $\frac{1}{3}$ of the field or $\frac{1}{4}$?*

3 For older children, write the fractional number $\frac{1}{3}$ on the chalkboard. Explain that the 3 tells how many equal parts the whole is divided into and the 1 tells how many of those parts you are talking about. *How would we write one fourth? One half?* Have volunteers demonstrate.

4 *Ready for another problem? A class has a new, very long rope to cut up for jump ropes. At first they decide to make two equal pieces. Then someone suggests making three equal pieces. "It might make four jump ropes," someone else says.*

5 Tell the children they are going to find out what some pieces of yarn look like if they are cut into 2, 3, or 4 equal parts. Have the children predict which pieces will be the longest, the halves, thirds, or fourths.

6 Distribute four lengths of yarn, scissors, glue, and construction paper to each pair. *When you find the parts of the yarn, make a display on the paper that shows a whole length, and $\frac{1}{2}$, $\frac{1}{3}$, and $\frac{1}{4}$. Remember to make equal parts.*

> Watch as the children find the fractional parts. Finding thirds is not easy. Make note of ways children approach this task. You might have younger children do the two problems on this page on different days.

7 Bring children together to discuss their displays. *How did you find the equal parts? Was one of them harder to find than the others? Which part is larger, $\frac{1}{2}$, $\frac{1}{3}$, or $\frac{1}{4}$?*

MathLand® Smart Strands • Grades K–2
© Creative Publications

Today we design trains and use fractions to describe them. We may be in for a surprise!

1 Have the children sit in a circle on the rug. Spread out 100 LinkerCubes in each of two colors so that all the children can reach them. ***Today we're going to design "number 4 trains."*** Show a train made with two yellow and two green cubes. ***I'd like everyone to create a number 4 train made with two colors.***

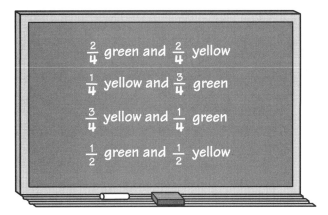

$\frac{2}{4}$ green and $\frac{2}{4}$ yellow

$\frac{1}{4}$ yellow and $\frac{3}{4}$ green

$\frac{3}{4}$ yellow and $\frac{1}{4}$ green

$\frac{1}{2}$ green and $\frac{1}{2}$ yellow

For younger children, you may wish to use whole numbers to describe trains throughout this activity. For example, "1 out of 4 parts is green." For older children who have not been introduced to fraction notation, write $\frac{2}{4}$ on the board as you describe your train in step 2. Explain that the 4 tells how many equal parts the whole is divided into and the 2 tells how many of those parts you are talking about.

2 ***Let's use fractions to describe the trains you've designed. My train is $\frac{2}{4}$ green and $\frac{2}{4}$ yellow. Does anyone else have a train that is $\frac{2}{4}$ green and $\frac{2}{4}$ yellow?*** Have the children put those trains in the middle of the circle. Write the description on the chalkboard. (Children may suggest using $\frac{1}{2}$ to talk about these trains as well. Tell them that while that is correct, for today we will describe trains in terms of fourths.)

3 ***Let's hear about the other trains that were made. Can you use fractions to tell about those trains?*** Add children's responses on the board.

4 ***Let's design number 4 trains that have three colors.*** Add 100 LinkerCubes of a third color to the cubes already out. Place some of each color at desks for children to work with. Each train should have a different fraction description. Children should write the descriptions on paper, and save the trains on their desks to be shared later.

5 When the children have finished making three-color trains, have the class discuss their results. ***How many different trains were you able to make?*** Call on children one at a time to show a train and write one of the three possible descriptions on the board. Ask children to hold up trains that fit each description.

Children may be surprised to find there are only three fraction descriptions possible. Each train will have two cubes of one color and one each of the other two colors. Children should notice that the *arrangements* of the cubes can be different for trains with the same description. Some children may enjoy the challenge of finding all the different looking three-color trains they can make that fit one description.

We explore equal parts of Pattern Blocks. We can use the blocks to show halves, thirds, and sixths.

1 Have collections of Pattern Blocks in easy reach of children as they work in pairs on today's problems. ***Take a yellow block. Can you find another block that is $\frac{1}{2}$ of the yellow block?*** Give children time to figure out that the red block is half. Then have them explain how they know it is half.

2 ***Can you find a block that is $\frac{1}{3}$ of the yellow block?*** Give pairs time to determine that the blue block is a third. Have them tell why they know it is a third.

Marisa	The red block is $\frac{1}{2}$ because two of them equal the yellow block.
Kevin	Three blue blocks cover the yellow block, and all blue blocks are the same size, so blue is $\frac{1}{3}$ of yellow.

3 ***Work with your partner to find blocks that show equal parts of other Pattern Blocks. Pick one Pattern Block to start. Try to find more than one way to make equal parts for that block. Then choose another block and do the same. Save the parts you find on your desk so we can share them later.***

4 When children have investigated many of the blocks, have them stop and share their findings with the class. Children can check the displays on their own desks to verify the findings others report.

5 Model the number sentences that tell about the children's findings. On the chalkboard, write $\frac{1}{3} + \frac{1}{3} + \frac{1}{3} = 1$, and read it with the class. ***This number sentence tells about some of the block parts you've shown on your desks. Which are those?*** Children may report finding thirds for the hexagon and trapezoid. Repeat this process for $\frac{1}{2} + \frac{1}{2} = 1$, and $\frac{1}{6} + \frac{1}{6} + \frac{1}{6} + \frac{1}{6} + \frac{1}{6} + \frac{1}{6} = 1$.

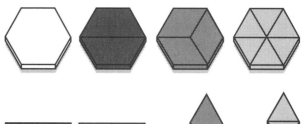

Interview Assessment	As the children work today, approach individual children and say, ***Tell me about the equal parts you're finding. How do you know that's [a sixth]?***

Can we use what we know about fractions to tell how much pizza was eaten last night?

1 On the overhead projector, draw five-eighths of a circle as shown below. *Last night I bought a pizza. This morning there was this much left. What fraction of the pizza was left over?* Give pairs time to discuss the problem, then take responses. Children may come to the overhead to draw as they explain their thinking. *What fraction of the pizza did I eat?*

2 Write the fraction $\frac{3}{8}$ and ask children what each digit means. The discussion should clarify that the 8 tells how many equal parts the whole is divided into and the 3 tells how many of those parts you are talking about.

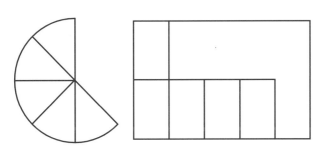

3 On the overhead projector, draw a rectangle. Then draw 5 of 10 equal parts, as shown above. Include the outline of the rectangle. *My friend made a chocolate cake in a pan. She cut it into equal parts. After dessert, there was this much left. Use a fraction to tell what part of the cake was eaten.*

4 Let pairs talk and draw to solve the problem, then discuss their answers with the class. The discussion is likely to bring out the point that $\frac{5}{10}$ and $\frac{1}{2}$ are both correct ways to tell how much was eaten. Review how these fractions are written.

5 *Now it's your turn to write "fraction leftovers problems" for us to solve. What are some foods you could write about?* On chart paper make a list of children's suggestions. Children may write problems individually or in pairs.

6 Toward the middle of math time, have children exchange problems to solve. They should make a recording that shows and tells about their thinking. If time permits, or on another day, have children continue to exchange and solve each other's problems.

7 Bring the class together to share the problems they worked on and their solutions. The children might like to bind their problems into a book and place it in the class library.

Home Work

At home, have children write a leftovers problem and ask a family member to solve it.

Farm Fractions

Equal-size parts are what we look for this week as we explore strategies for identifying parts of a set as fractions. We use our intuitive ways of thinking to solve problems involving common fractions. The special ways we learn to talk about fractions and write about them help us communicate about parts of sets.

Key Mathematical Ideas

★ When a set of things is broken up into equal parts, each part is a fraction of the set.

★ Fractional parts may be equal parts of a whole or of a set.

★ Special language and terms are helpful for describing and naming the equal parts of sets.

★ There may be more than one way to name fractional parts of a set.

Prior Knowledge

These activities can serve as introductions to fractions. Children will bring to this work their informal experiences out of school with sets of things and with situations that call for fair shares.

WHAT THE CHILDREN WILL DO

- Solve problems involving common fractions

- Use a variety of approaches, including drawing and using objects, to find fractional parts of sets

- Describe parts of a set using pairs of whole numbers

- Name fractional parts of a set using fraction terms and symbols

Getting Ready

Materials

- LinkerCubes or Rainbow Tiles

- Half sheets of paper

- Chart paper

- 11" × 17" drawing paper

- Overhead LinkerCubes

Preparation

 • Obtain the book, *Give Me Half,* by Stuart Murphy (HarperCollins Books, 1996). For Day Trip Two, collect egg cartons, one per pair. For Day Trip Three, copy Scarecrows (page 94) one per child. For Day Trip Five, copy Harvest Time (page 95) for each pair.

Pigs like to eat corn. Farmer Jane has to make sure each pig gets an equal part.

1 *Farmer Jane is going to feed her pigs. She has 6 large ears of corn. There are 2 pigs waiting at the trough. "That's easy," says Farmer Jane. "Each pig gets half the corn." How many ears of corn will each pig get?* Discuss the answer with the class.

2 *Before she could feed the two pigs, another pig joined them. "Now there are 3 pigs. Each pig gets one third of the corn,"* thought Farmer Jane. "I wonder how many ears of corn each pig will get now." Give children time to solve the problem. Some children may use LinkerCubes, some children may draw, and others may solve the problem mentally.

3 When children have solved the problem, have them share and discuss their solutions.

Do you all agree that each pig gets 2 out of 6 ears?	
Marisa	Each pig gets 2 because 2 plus 2 plus 2 is 6.
Jeremy	We got 6 cubes and put 1 cube out for each pig. Then there were enough for each pig to get 1 more.

The book, *Give Me Half*, by Stuart Murphy, is an excellent starting point for discussing equal parts of sets. You might begin today's activity by reading it to the class. In the story, two children share a package of two cupcakes. Each child gets one cupcake, or one half of the cupcakes.

4 You might choose to extend older children's thinking by posing the following problem for them to solve. *Farmer Jane wants to do some planning. She has 3 pigs all together. What size groups of corn ears will work when she wants to give each pig a third of the ears? She wants to make bunches of whole ears of corn, and she doesn't want any ears left over. Will a group of 11 ears work?* Give children time to answer this question, then discuss their reasoning.

5 *With your partner, find some numbers of corn ears that Farmer Jane can use to give each pig one third of the ears. Record your findings.*

6 Bring the children together to share their recordings and discuss their findings. *How did you figure out what numbers of ears of corn would work?*

There are 12 eggs in a dozen, and there are lots of recipes that call for eggs. Today, we do some planning in the kitchen.

1 Show the class a closed egg carton. ***What can you tell me about what I'm holding?*** Write the class's responses on chart paper. Then distribute an egg carton to each pair. ***Look inside and on the carton. Did you find any new information to add to the chart?*** Make sure all children know there are 12 eggs in a dozen.

egg carton

holds 12 eggs

holds a dozen eggs

buy at grocery store

2 ***I'm having company this weekend. I need 6 eggs to make omelets. I have a full carton of eggs in my refrigerator. What part of the eggs will I use?*** Let pairs talk about the problem, then discuss the answer with the class.

Some children may use the language "6 out of the 12 eggs." Others may use the language "one half of the eggs, or half a dozen." You can introduce language with questions such as, ***Six out of 12 eggs are used. Is there another way to say that? Can you use a fraction to name the part that I will use?***

3 ***Here's a problem. Farmer Jane is making pancakes for her family. The recipe calls for 3 eggs. She has a full carton of eggs. What part of those eggs does she need? Find the answer. Then draw and tell about your thinking.***

4 Children may work in pairs or individually. LinkerCubes or Rainbow Tiles should be available for children who choose to use them.

5 When children have had time to solve the problem and record their solutions, bring them together. Have children share all the different ways they worked on the problem. Children may say Farmer Jane used one fourth or a fourth of the eggs.

6 Extend the children's thinking by posing the problem, ***How many batches of pancakes can Farmer Jane make with one dozen eggs?*** Give children time to think about the problem, then have them share their solutions.

Look at all the scarecrows. No two are alike, but it's pretty easy to see that 4 out of 8 of them are wearing overalls. That's $\frac{1}{2}$!

1 *Have you ever seen a scarecrow?* Take children's responses. Children may connect scarecrows with Halloween or ways they're portrayed in books. The class may be interested in doing some research to find out more.

2 Distribute a copy of Scarecrows (page 94) to each child. *There's a scarecrow competition at the county fair. Farmer Jane wants to tell her friends about the scarecrows. She thinks to herself, "Half the scarecrows are wearing overalls."* (With younger children, use the language, "Four out of eight scarecrows are wearing overalls.")

Do you agree?

Mikiko   I agree. Four out of 8 scarecrows are wearing overalls, and 4 is half of 8.

Robbie   I also agree. I matched each one with overalls with one with pants, and it came out even. It made two equal groups.

---

3 Some older children may suggest it can also be said that four eighths of the scarecrows are wearing overalls. Let the children discuss this idea. *Are both expressions correct?*

4 If children have not been introduced to the way fractions are written, explain the notation as you write both fractions, $\frac{1}{2}$ and $\frac{4}{8}$. *For $\frac{1}{2}$, we say "one out of two."— Which number, the 1 or the 2, tells how many equal parts there are all together? Which number tells how many halves there are?* Use the same process to talk about $\frac{4}{8}$.

5 *What other true statements can we make?* Take several responses, writing them on the board. For older children, review the fraction notation you use. Then ask the class to explain why they agree or disagree with each statement.

6 *With your partner, write some more true statements about the scarecrows.* For younger children, write the expression, ___ out of ___, on the board to help them use this language.

7 At the end of math time, bring children together to share their recordings. Ask the class whether they agree with each statement shared.

Home Work   Children can write about "Family Fractions" at home. Discuss beforehand some of the things they might report, such as, $\frac{1}{2}$ of the family are kids, $\frac{1}{4}$ go to school, $\frac{3}{4}$ were born in this country, $\frac{4}{4}$ like ice cream.

Planning a garden gets us thinking about parts again. What part of the garden should we plant in tomatoes?

1 Have children discuss their experiences gardening. ***Have you ever planted a garden? Did you plan what seeds to plant in certain places?***

2 ***Farmer Jane needs some help with her garden. She has 12 rows ready to plant. All the rows are the same length, and she's going to plant one kind of vegetable in each row. Suppose she wanted to plant half her garden in tomatoes, how many rows would that be?*** Discuss the problem with the class. Let children draw on the board or use manipulatives to model the problem and explain their thinking to the class.

3 ***Farmer Jane has made a list of her other decisions about the garden.*** Read the list below with the class as you write it on chart paper.

4 ***Help Farmer Jane by drawing a plan of one way she could plant the 12 rows of her garden. On another piece of paper, tell how many rows she should plant of each vegetable.*** Remind children to plan just one type of vegetable for each row. To help children get started, ask questions such as, $\frac{1}{3}$ *of 12 rows is how many rows?*

5 Distribute 11" × 17" paper to pairs for their drawings. Have crayons or colored pens available.

6 At the end of math time, have children discuss their plans. ***How did you decide how many rows to plant of each vegetable? For which vegetables was it easy to plan? Were there some for which it was harder? Should all your plans look exactly the same? Why or why not?***

Children's responses will vary. Some children may have the three rows of tomatoes right next to each other, while other children may alternate the rows of vegetables. Either plan is acceptable as long as the child has depicted the correct number of rows of each vegetable.

Garden

$\frac{1}{3}$ tomatoes

$\frac{1}{4}$ squash

$\frac{1}{6}$ carrots

$\frac{1}{6}$ lettuce

$\frac{1}{12}$ cucumbers

We put our fraction know-how to use. Would we rather have $\frac{1}{2}$ of 4 tomatoes, or $\frac{1}{3}$ of 9 tomatoes?

1 At the overhead projector, use Overhead LinkerCubes to show an array of 4 and an array of 9 red tiles. *Farmer Jane is harvesting her vegetables and packing them in trays. If she asked you, "Which is more, $\frac{1}{2}$ of 4 tomatoes, or $\frac{1}{3}$ of 9 tomatoes?" what would you say?* Write the question on the board.

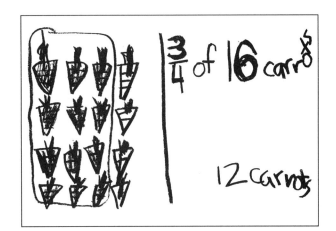

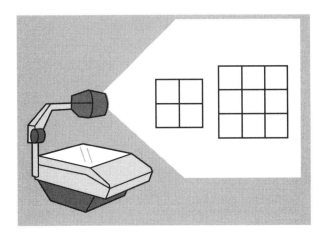

2 Have pencils, paper, and LinkerCubes available for pairs to use as they work on this problem. Then have children share their thinking with the class. Invite them to the overhead to demonstrate as they explain.

3 Distribute a copy of Harvest Time to each pair. *Now it's time to answer other Which is more? questions.* Have children work individually or in pairs to find the answer to each question and then record their answers on half sheets of paper. LinkerCubes should be available for children's use.

4 At the end of math time, bring the children together to share their experiences solving the problems. Children can show their solutions on the overhead projector. *Was the answer always the one you expected when you first read the question? Were some problems harder than others? Did you all solve the problems the same way?*

Interview Assessment	As the children work today, approach individual children and say, *Tell me about the problem you're working on. Which fraction is more?*

Spatial Sensibility

This week, we will be using real objects in our environment as well as creating shapes of our own. We'll use our spatial sense and creativity to make symmetrical creatures, build three-dimensional models, and solve number riddles. Along the way, we'll learn some important vocabulary.

Key Mathematical Ideas

★ Shapes are found in our environment.

★ You can make models and new shapes out of existing shapes.

★ Mathematical language is important for describing our physical surroundings.

★ A number line is helpful for finding missing numbers.

Prior Knowledge

Children should be familiar with names of common shapes and with ordinal numbers. They should be able to cut straight and curved lines and also have experience drawing a straight line using a straightedge.

WHAT THE CHILDREN WILL DO

• Describe objects using informal positional language

• Make figures with line symmetry

• Cut geometric shapes apart and identify new shapes

• Use whole numbers to locate points on a number line

Getting Ready

Materials

• Teddy Bear or Dinosaur counters, 1 per child

• Geoblocks or Table Blocks, 5 per pair of children

• full sheets of paper, 1 per child

• construction paper

• file folders, or piece of stiff cardboard, 1 per pair

• scissors

• straightedges

• small mirrors (optional)

• glue

Preparation

• For Day Trip One, collect containers such as margarine tubs or small empty boxes (1 per child). On Day Trip Two, you will need whole sheets and scraps of construction paper. For Day Trip Three, draw a picture frame like the one on page 37 and make a copy for each child. For Day Trip Five, you'll need at least one copy of Number Line (page 96) per child.

Today we'll brainstorm positional words and try our hand at creating and describing some situations with bears (or dinosaurs) and the huts they live in.

1 Gather children in an area where everyone can see you and the easel (or some other prop). Stand in front of the easel. ***Look at me and look at the easel. Where am I standing?*** Fill in this sentence. (_Teacher's name_) is (_in front of_) the easel. Move to different positions such as beside and behind, to give children more practice with positional words. Write these words on the board.

2 ***We call these positional words. Can we add any more to our list?*** Add any obvious ones that may have been missed.

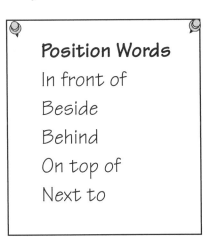

> ### Position Words
> In front of
> Beside
> Behind
> On top of
> Next to

3 ***Let's practice positional words all together.*** Pass out one Teddy Bear or Dinosaur counter to each child. Also give each child one container such as an empty margarine tub, or a small box. Hold up a container. ***We'll call this our hut. As I call out the position, you put your counter where you think it should go. The bear is inside the hut.***

4 Call out a variety of positions to give the class substantial practice, then invite children to suggest their own situations. You may want to have children practice filling in a sentence that is modeled on the board. (*The bear is ___ the hut.*)

5 On a piece of paper, have children draw a few pictures that show their dinosaur or bear in different positions. Invite children to write a sentence or two describing the positions in relation to the hut.

6 After each child has made several pictures, staple the recordings together to make a small book. Have children read their books to each other to provide more experiences using positional language.

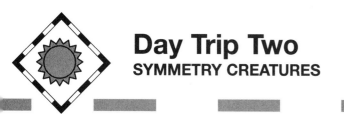
Today we're going to fold and cut out a symmetrical shape and create a symmetrical creature. It's a good day to get out your art scrap box.

1 Gather children around you as you demonstrate folding and cutting. *Today we are going to create some interesting creatures. We'll call them "symmetrical creatures."* While children are watching, demonstrate folding the paper, drawing interesting designs with a pencil on one side of the fold, and then cutting.

2 *What do you notice about the shape that I have cut out?* Cut out two more and then point out the line of symmetry. *This line shows that the shape is the same on both sides.* Discuss the idea that the shapes are "balanced," or have equal sides. *We call these shapes symmetrical. Look around the room; do you see other objects that look symmetrical to you?*

3 Children should notice that the two sides are a reflection of each other. They can refold their creature to check if it is symmetrical, or you can supply mirrors for the children to check the reflection.

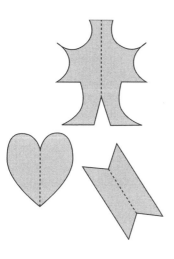

4 *Now let's make these shapes into creatures. Using scrap paper, cut out eyes, ears, and other features to make these creatures more interesting. Because they are symmetrical, you will need to cut out two of everything. If the creature has a stripe on one side of the line, there must be a stripe on the other side of the line, too.* Demonstrate how to cut two exact items by cutting through two pieces at once.

5 Hand out materials to children and let them begin working. Remind children to make sure the two sides are reflections of each other. You may want to create a bulletin board titled "Symmetrical Creatures" to display the work.

Math Journal

Ask children to draw an example of a symmetrical creature that they made today. *Show its line of symmetry.*

Today we'll be drawing portraits to demonstrate that shapes are found within shapes.

1 Distribute the picture frame sheets you have prepared. Discuss what picture children might want to draw. You may want to direct the topic for the picture to relate to a current classroom theme. Allow time for drawing and coloring and then bring the group back together. (You may want to recommend that children don't get too attached to their drawings because they will be cutting them into pieces later on.)

2 *Now let's pretend that this picture is not made of paper, but of glass. Oops! I accidentally dropped it. What would happen? That's right, it would break into smaller pieces—or shapes. Would the shapes be large or small? Would they all be the same? Think about what yours might look like.*

3 *First cut the picture frame out of the paper. Now turn your picture over and start drawing lines on the back of your picture to make smaller shapes. Use a straightedge or a ruler to help you draw straight lines. Try making shapes that you know about, such as triangles and rectangles. After you have the whole picture divided up, cut each piece apart.*

4 After children have had time to cut their pieces have them lay the pieces out on their desks. Pose questions such as, *Who can hold up a rectangle? Who has a large triangle? Who has a shape with more than four sides?* For fun have the children exchange puzzles and put each other's together.

Interview Assessment

As children are working, approach individuals and ask questions to check their understanding of shapes. *What shapes did you make? What shape do the pieces make if you put them back together?*

On this day we'll notice and describe three-dimensional objects, and then play a game to practice the positional words we learned in Day Trip One.

1 Find an example of an object in a book such as a lunch box or a block, then find a real example of that object in your classroom. Compare the differences. Discuss properties of three-dimensional objects. (They have more than one surface; they have corners and edges; they have thickness.)

2 *Now look around the classroom. What other three-dimensional objects catch your eye? Today we're going to play a game with some other three-dimensional objects.*

3 Show children your collection of Geoblocks or Table Blocks. Hold up a cube and ask a child to describe it. *What can we say about this block? How many corners does it have? How many faces (flat surfaces)? What shape are they?* Practice with a few more blocks, encouraging children to use mathematical language as they describe them.

4 Distribute the blocks so that each pair of children has an identical set of five blocks. Have pairs set up a file folder wall, and then explain the rules for Behind the Wall.

5 You may want to model describing a construction, reminding children of the positional language they practiced in Day Trip One.

Behind the Wall

1. Players sit facing one another with a file folder forming a wall between them.

2. One player makes a block design.

3. The second player tries to make the same design from verbal instructions given by the first player.

4. When the players are ready, they lift the wall and compare designs.

5. Players reverse roles and play again.

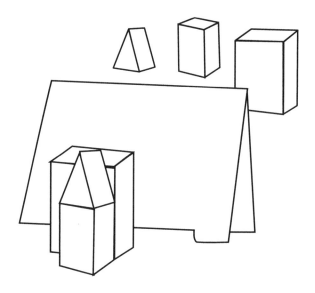

Home Work Have each child find one three-dimensional item at home. In class, children can describe their items to the others.

In this Day Trip we'll be using a number line to locate whole numbers. Not only is this a good activity for finding and naming number positions, it is an excellent way to practice listening skills.

1 Hand out a blank number line for each child. Discuss what a number line is and what is different about this number line. (It doesn't have numbers on it.) ***What could we use this number line for? How would we use it?***

2 Tape or glue together the ends to make one long number line. ***The numbers are missing on this number line because we will be filling them in. I will be giving you clues to certain numbers and you will write the number after you've heard the riddle. Where does the number line start?***

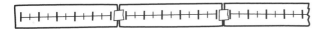

Because there are no numbers on the number line, it can start at zero or it can start at twenty. You will need to guide those decisions based on the abilities of the group you are teaching, or perhaps the children can help you decide the beginning and ending numbers.

3 ***I'm thinking of a number that is 5 more than 6. How do we know where to write it on the line? Who would like to show me how to find where we should write it?*** Invite children to share their strategies. ***I'm thinking of a number that's greater than 5, and has two digits that add up to 3. How will the first number we wrote help us to find the new number?***

4 After you have said a few riddles, have children think up their own. If possible, have the children write them down. Then have children tell their clues to a partner. Children may want to use extra number lines to solve each other's riddles. You can write a collection of riddles on chart paper to be solved throughout the week.

5 This is an activity that can be done throughout the year. As the children's math skills grow, the riddles can become more difficult.

Side Trip

Roll a Number

Children might like to invent number-line games using numbered cubes. For example, put a marker at the beginning of the number line. Roll the cube. If it's an even number, move forward. If it's an odd number, you lose your turn.

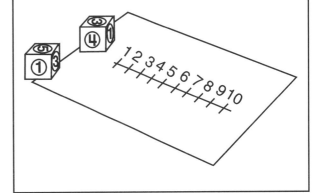

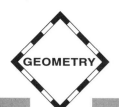

Investigating Shapes

This week we'll work with geometry in a number of ways. Our visual skills will be challenged as we look for shapes in the environment. We'll also study cylinders, look for rules in groups of shapes, and identify open and closed shapes.

Key Mathematical Ideas

★ Linear and solid shapes are found in our environment.

★ Shapes are made of other shapes.

★ Attributes can be used to describe and sort shapes.

Prior Knowledge

Children should be able to identify basic geometric shapes such as triangles, squares, rectangles, and circles. They should be able to follow step-by-step directions.

WHAT THE CHILDREN WILL DO

- Identify shapes in the environment
- Identify and make cylinders
- Make figures on Geoboards
- Write clues to describe shapes
- Recognize open and closed figures

Getting Ready

Materials

- Attribute Blocks

- Geoboards and rubber bands (optional)

- Colored construction paper, 9" × 12"

- Half-sheets of white paper

- Tape or glue

- Scissors

- String or yarn

Preparation

 • For Day Trips One and Four, prepare ten half sheets of paper per student. For Day Trip Three, prepare copies of Geoboard Dot Paper (page 108) and Matching Shapes (page 97). For Day Trip Five, cut a three foot piece of yarn for each child and make copies of 2-cm Dot Paper (page 98).

Today we'll be going on a walk to look for shapes in the environment. We will also be categorizing pictures of shapes.

1 *Today I am going to draw some shapes you may know.* Draw a square, circle, rectangle, and triangle on chart paper. *Now I'll draw some shapes you may not know.* Draw a trapezoid, hexagon, and rhombus. *Tell me what you know about these shapes. I'll write what you tell me next to each shape.* Encourage students to talk about the sides and corners and how they relate to each other.

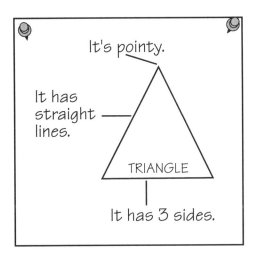

2 *Let's find examples of these shapes around our classroom.* Children can walk around the room for a few minutes. *What shapes did you find?*

3 *Next, we are going to take a walk around the playground and look for shapes. What shape do you think you will see a lot? What shape do you think might be harder to find?*

4 During the walk, ask children to point out items such as signs, ladders, play structures, basketball hoops, painted lines, and other natural contexts for shapes. Encourage children to describe the shapes they see in balls, boxes, shapes, and cones.

5 After the walk, children can discuss the shapes they found. *Let's make charts that show examples of the shapes we found on or near the playground.* Divide the class into small groups. You can assign each group a shape chart, or let groups contribute to all of the charts. *Think of what you saw on the playground that you can add to the shape charts. Draw a picture and then tape it under the correct shape on our class chart.*

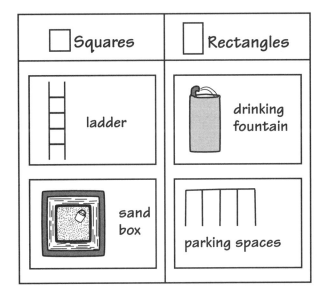

6 *What shape did we see the most? What shape did we see the least? Was there anything that fit on more than one chart?* Children may also cut out pictures from magazines and add them to the charts. The charts will be useful for future discussions about shapes.

Today we'll make a decorative mobile to help us get acquainted with cylinders and practice identifying shapes.

1 Gather examples of cylinders to share with the class. You may include paper towel rolls, film containers, cans, and jars to show some everyday items. Share some pictures from magazines and books showing cylinders.

2 *What are some things that we know about cylinders? I'll write them down as you tell me.*

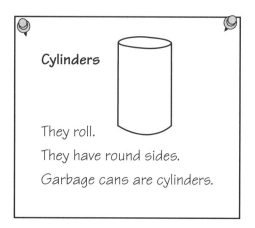

Cylinders

They roll.

They have round sides.

Garbage cans are cylinders.

3 *Today you are going to make a Shape Mobile. The largest part of the mobile is a cylinder.* Distribute 9" × 12" pieces of construction paper. *How can we change this paper to make it into a cylinder?* Have children try to form the paper into a cylinder. *That's right, roll it and we'll tape the ends together.*

4 *Now that we've made a cylinder, let's add other shapes.* Children can trace shapes using items around the room or trace Attribute Blocks. Encourage the class to draw a variety of shapes that they are familiar with. *Cut out the shapes and glue a few on the cylinder.*

5 Next, help children punch holes in the remaining shapes and around the bottom of the cylinder. *Tie the shapes to the cylinder with string.* To hang the mobile, punch two holes at the top of the cylinder. Loop a string through the holes and tie each end as shown.

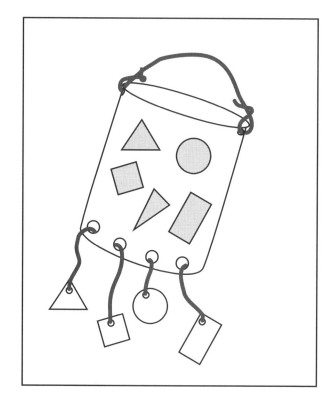

Interview Assessment

As children are making their mobiles, ask questions such as, *What is the name of this shape? Which shape has three sides? Which shape is the same as a wheel?*

Today we'll be working with re-creating shapes using our Geoboards and dot paper. Then, we'll see what the shapes have in common.

1 Distribute Dot Paper (page 108), one for each student. (You may use Geoboards and rubber-bands if available.) ***Today we'll play a matching game. I will make a shape on my Geoboard and then you draw the same shape on your Dot Paper.*** Demonstrate three different triangles. ***What did my three shapes have in common?***

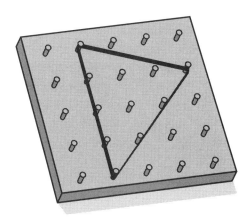

2 Children should try to make their shapes the same as yours. To help them out, you may want them to count how many pegs each shape touches or encloses.

Geometry helps us represent, and describe in an orderly manner, the world in which we live. One way to help children make these connections is by having them compare shapes to familiar items in their lives. Sentence starters such as, ***It looks like a*** ___, or ***it reminds me of*** ___, allow children to make these connections.

3 Distribute Matching Shapes (page 97). ***On the left side of the paper you will see some shapes. Your job is to use a pencil to draw the same figures on the right side.***

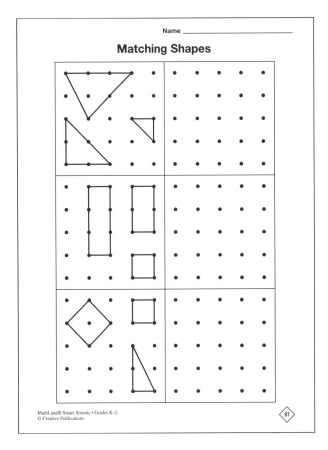

4 After children have had time to work, ask, ***Can you see what the three shapes in the first box have in common?***

- ***What about the second box?***

- ***What shape was the easiest to draw?***

- ***What shape took the longest to draw?***

- ***Did counting the pegs help you?***

- ***Can you make a circle on the Geoboard Dot Paper?***

Day Trip Four
SHAPE RIDDLES

Today we think of ways to describe shapes and play a riddle game.

1 *Let's play a game. I am thinking of a shape that has three corners. What shape am I thinking of?* Do a few more shape riddles in this format. *I am thinking of a shape that is the top of an ice cream cone. The shape has no straight edges or corners.*

2 *Now each of you is going to be describing three shapes in your own words.* Hand out seven half-sheets of paper per child. *Trace around one Attribute Block on one piece of paper.* Older children can make a different shape using more than one Attribute Block.

3 *On another piece of paper, write one or more sentence clues that describe the shape.* You may want to provide a list of descriptive words that children can use to write the clues.

4 After everyone has traced three shapes and written three clues, staple the pages together to make booklets. Follow each clue with the page with the matching shape. Children can make a cover with the title, "Guess My Shape."

5 Have pairs share their booklets and try to guess the shapes.

- *Which shapes were difficult to guess?*

- *Which shapes were easy to figure out?*

- *What clues helped you the most?*

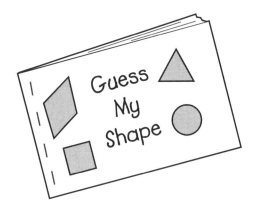

Home Work   Have children read their shape books to someone in their family. Can the family members guess the shapes correctly?

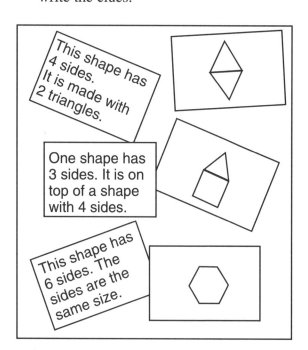

This shape has 4 sides. It is made with 2 triangles.

One shape has 3 sides. It is on top of a shape with 4 sides.

This shape has 6 sides. The sides are the same size.

MathLand® Smart Strands • Grades K–2
© Creative Publications

Today we'll experiment with open and closed figures.

1 Draw several open and several closed figures on the chalkboard or easel. ***Who can tell me the difference between the two sets of figures that I have drawn?***

2 Discuss open and closed figures. ***Use your hands to show me a closed figure. Now use your hands to show me an open figure. Explain to a partner the differences between open and closed figures.***

3 Distribute a piece of yarn to each child. ***With your piece of yarn, make a closed figure with four corners. Make an open figure with at least two straight lines. Make an open figure with one corner. Make a closed figure with three corners. Experiment and make more shapes with your yarn.***

4 ***Now let's play the game Dot-to-Dot.*** Hand out 2-cm dot paper to each pair of children.

Dot-to-Dot

1. When it's your turn, draw a line from one dot to another dot. Each line needs to be attached to another line.

2. If you make a closed figure, write the first letter of your name inside the shape.

3. The closed figures do not have to be squares or "boxes," they may be other shapes, too. (Older children can use diagonal lines; younger children may try to make only squares or rectangles.)

4. The player with more closed figures is the winner.

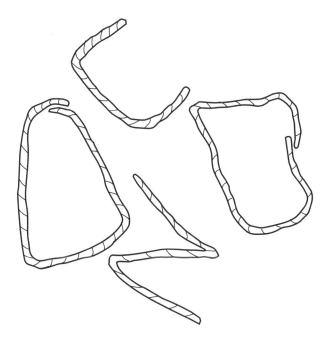

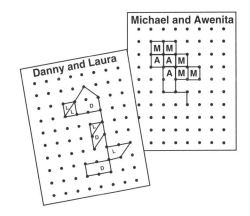

Math Journal

Draw some open and closed figures in your journal. Describe the figures.

Measurement Hunts

This week children will learn about customary and metric measurement units. The children will find items that are approximately equal in length to an inch and to a centimeter. Later they will measure items using those units. Children will also identify items that weigh about a pound and items that weigh about a kilogram. Finally the children will use these measurements to solve some problems in the classroom.

Key Mathematical Ideas

★ We can use "found" measures to approximate distances and weights.

★ A standard system of measurement allows people to communicate information about measurement accurately.

★ Units in a system can be expressed in terms of other units in a system; for example, twelve inches equal one foot.

Prior Knowledge

Children should understand what it means when something is longer or shorter than something else. They should recognize when something is heavier or lighter than something else. Children need to have counting ability and the spatial skills necessary to line items up next to each other.

WHAT THE CHILDREN WILL DO

- Discover "found" measures that help them to estimate the length and weight of different objects

- Explore the relationship between the size of a unit of measure and the number of units needed to measure a given object

- Solve measurement problems

Getting Ready

Materials

- Easy Scale or Primary Balance, 1 per group if possible

- rulers (metric and standard)

Preparation

- Prepare copies of Measurement Hunt (page 99), at least four per child. For Day Trip One, cut one-inch squares of paper for each child. For Day Trip Two, you need one centimeter cube. For Day Trip Three, make sure there is a model of a pound for each group of children. Use a pound of rice, or combine items in a bag until it approximates one pound. For Day Trip Four, make sure there is a model of a kilogram for each group of children.

MathLand® Smart Strands • Grade K–2
© Creative Publications

We start out with an inch hunt while we think about how we measure distances.

1 *Today we are going to measure our desks. Does anyone have any ideas how we can measure how long it is?* Suggest that children use their fists, end to end, to measure their desks. *How many fists do you think it is from one end to the other?* Have children estimate and then measure their desks using their fists.

2 As children finish measuring, have them report their measurement to you. Make a chart on the board to record the measures. *Why do the numbers differ?*

Number of Fists	Number of Children
25	2
26	1
27	0
28	5
29	6

3 Questions like the following can help children understand that a standardized system is necessary to communicate measurements.

- *If you were talking to someone on the phone could you explain how long the desk is?*

- *If that person was going to bring a tablecloth to fit the desk, what would you say?*

4 Children will probably suggest that a standard measurement system is needed. Show them a piece of paper or a drawing on the board that is about an inch square. *What do people use inches for?*

5 *Now we're going to hunt for things that are about an inch long.* (It might be helpful to put out more items that approximate an inch, such as paper clips and math manipulatives.) Distribute inch-square pieces of paper and the Measurement Hunt recording sheet. Have the children draw a one-inch line segment at the top of the page. Tell them to look for items they think are about an inch, check them against their model, then list them on their recording sheet.

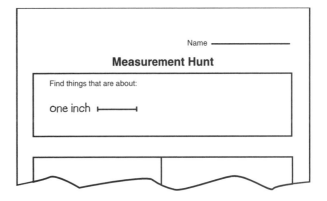

6 Have children share the results of their inch hunt. *How did you know if something was one inch long?*

7 Ask children how they might use the inch to solve the problem of measuring desks. This idea will be explored further in Day Trip Two.

Day Trip Two
MEETING THE CENTIMETER

Building on our experiences with the inch, we learn to measure centimeters—this time using rulers.

1 Remind children about Day Trip One and the problem of measuring a desk using the inch. *How could we measure longer items, like the chalkboard or the length of the classroom?* Have children examine their rulers. *Can you find an inch on your ruler? Does anyone know how long the whole ruler is?*

2 Hold up a centimeter cube. *This cube is one centimeter on each edge. Can you find one centimeter on your ruler?* Explain that there are two main measurement systems, the metric and the U. S. customary. The centimeter is part of the metric system.

3 Tell children they are going to have another measurement hunt, but this time they're going to look for things that are five centimeters long. Distribute new recording sheets and model how to write "5 centimeters." *Use the ruler to draw a five-centimeter segment at the top of the page. Remember to record the items you find that are about five centimeters long.*

4 When children are finished hunting have them share their findings. *Did you find things that were more than five centimeters long? Less than five centimeters?* Invite children to pick a given number of centimeters, for example 8 or 12, and have them draw a line of that length on a new recording sheet. Then have them hunt for items in the room that are about that length.

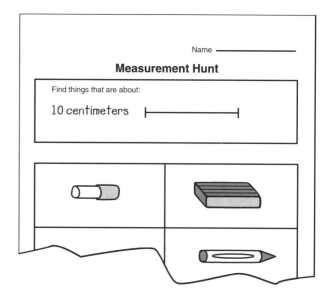

Name ——————

Measurement Hunt

Find things that are about:

10 centimeters ├————————┤

5 Near the end of math time, gather the class together. *How could we measure the length of the classroom?* Have children talk about possible ways they might solve the problem. You might want to introduce the meter. Children might be interested to learn that there are 100 centimeters in a meter.

Math Journal

Have children tell how they might solve the problem of measuring the length of the classroom.

MathLand® Smart Strands • Grade K–2
© Creative Publications

We use the same strategies we used in Day Trips One and Two to start thinking about how we measure weight.

1 Ask children to tell about times that they have needed to know how much something weighs or why someone would need to know how much something weighs.

Eric	I need to know if it's too heavy for me to carry.
Melanie	The doctor wants to know how much I weigh.
George	My mom weighs the bananas in the store.

2 Show children the pound samples that you have prepared. Have groups of children take turns picking up the samples so they can get a feel for a pound.

3 *How could we tell if something weighs the same as a pound?* Have children share their ideas. Show children how they can hold the 1-pound item in one hand and can then lift the other item using their arms to feel if they are the same. While this is not an exact method, it is a good estimation technique.

Home Work

Send home Measurement Hunt recording sheets this week so children can list items that they think are one pound, five centimeters, and one inch.

4 Have children write "1 pound" at the top of a new Measurement Hunt recording sheet and try to find items that weigh a pound. You may wish to have children find a single item that is about a pound or several items they can easily band together with a rubber band. Another method is to give the children a bag and have them put items in it until the bag weighs about a pound. The children can take turns using the class standards to compare their items.

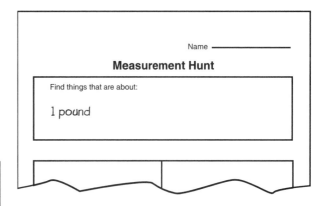

Name ————

Measurement Hunt

Find things that are about:

1 pound

5 Bring children together to share the results of their pound hunt. *How did you find items that weigh about one pound? How could you be sure?*

Today we go on a hunt for objects that weigh about one kilogram. This time we check our guesses using a balance scale.

1 Ask volunteers to help you review the pound hunt from Day Trip Three. *How did we find objects that weigh about one pound? What did we use to see if we were right?*

2 Ask children if they know of a more exact method of finding an object's weight. Introduce the Easy Scale or Primary Balance. Children can share any experiences they have had with the balance scale. Be sure to remind the class to use care in placing objects in the scale, in order to prolong the life of the scale.

3 *Today we're going on another measurement hunt. This time we're going to search for items that weigh about one kilogram. Can you name some items that are measured in kilograms?* (people, cars, and furniture) Show children the samples you have prepared that weigh about one kilogram. *How can I use the balance scale and this sample to find objects that weigh one kilogram?* Show children how to make the scale balance.

To introduce the concept of two different measurement systems, you can make a comparison with other countries that use a different kind of money than ours.

4 Distribute Measurement Hunt recording sheets and have children write "1 kilogram" in the top section. Have pairs of children hunt around the room for objects that weigh one kilogram. One method is to give each pair a bag and have them put items in it until the bag weighs about a kilogram. Children can check the bag using the simple balance and the kilogram sample weight.

For children who haven't had previous experience with balance scales, set up a station with a balance scale and various objects for children to explore during the week.

5 If time permits, and your children are ready, you can bring in a bathroom scale and have children estimate weights of different objects: for example something that weighs three pounds. Some bathroom scales measure in both kilograms and pounds. Have children estimate weights and then use the scale to check the results.

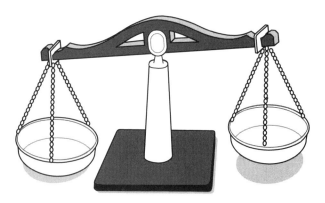

Children will use their measurement experiences from this week to solve some problems.

1 *Today is going to be a day of problem solving. You can use either the customary or the metric system to solve these puzzles, however it is best to choose one system and stick with it for a period of time.*

2 *First let's think through one problem together. How far is it from the door to the nearest desk?* Have children talk with a partner, discussing how they would solve the problem. Have pairs share their answers.

Celia	First we'd have to pick the closest desk and then use inches or feet.
Marisa	I think it should be feet, because inches are too small. We can use a ruler.

How long is the shortest pencil at your table? The longest?

How long is the longest book? The shortest one?

How tall is the teacher's chair? How tall is a child's chair?

Is the door wide enough to carry the desk through it?

When children line up to leave the room how long is the line?

If my backpack can only carry 5 pounds, can I carry home 5 books?

3 Once children have discussed their strategies, model how to measure the distance. Discuss with children some important things to do when measuring. *Why is it important to measure in a straight line?* You will probably want to return to these issues after children have had more experience in measuring.

4 Show children a list of measurement problems like those shown. Have children work in pairs to develop a plan for solving one of the problems. Children can draw a poster that shows their strategies. Remind them to identify which measuring tool they will use.

5 Bring children together to discuss their plans. Some strategies may lead to good discussion questions. *Can anyone think of an easier way to measure this distance?*

6 Invite children to revise their strategies before setting off to solve the problems. Pairs who are working on the same problem may want to compare their plans or work together.

Interview Assessment	As children are working on their problem-solving plans, ask individuals, *How did you decide on which measurement tool to use?*

How Much Does It Hold?

This week we explore capacity as we compare the sizes of different containers. We compare and order some containers by capacity. We end the week by learning something about the relationship between cups, pints, quarts, and gallons, and we also find out how much a liter is.

Key Mathematical Ideas

★ Selection of a measuring tool for a task depends upon the exactness of the measurement needed.

★ The capacity of a container can be described as the amount it holds.

★ There is a relationship between the different units used to describe measurements.

Prior Knowledge

This week's activities may be a first experience using standard units to measure capacity. Children should have some familiarity with terms in the U.S. customary measurement system, such as cup and quart. Also, children should have had the opportunity to explore other types of measurement such as length and weight in a variety of ways.

WHAT THE CHILDREN WILL DO

• Sort containers according to capacity

• Explore U.S. customary and metric measures

• Use 1-cup measures to find the capacity of different containers

Getting Ready

Materials

• chart paper

• full sheets of paper

• beans (about 3 cups per child)

• plastic 1-cup measure, 1 per pair

• box lid or large paper bag, 1 per pair

Preparation

 • Prior to this week, have children bring in containers of many sizes. Be sure to have at least two per child in a collection that includes at least one each: cup, half-pint, pint, quart, half-gallon, gallon, and liter. For Setting Out, bring in three coffee cups of different sizes. Create a spot in the classroom so the containers are available all week. For each table, fill a shoe box or bag with a supply of dried beans. For Looking Back, prepare copies of How Many Cups? (page 100), one per child.

We begin by looking at familiar objects—cups. How much is a cup? We decide there is good reason to have a standard measure.

1 As the class brings in their containers to add to the class collection, have them sort them into small and large containers. For today's activity, have each child choose a small container from the class collection. Each table of children should have a shoe box supply of beans to work with. Each pair should have a box lid or a small bag to keep track of their beans.

2 *How many handfuls of beans do you think it would take to fill up your container? Write down your prediction on a piece of scratch paper.*

3 Reminding children that the beans need to stay on the table, have them use the beans at the center of their table to fill their container, counting each handful. *Write down how many handfuls. Was your prediction close to the actual measurement?*

4 *If another child tried to fill your container, would she use the same number of handfuls? Trade containers with a partner and repeat the process.*

- *How many of my handfuls do you think it would take?*

- *Did it take more or fewer?*

5 *Imagine you are a chef, working in a restaurant. A recipe calls for one cup of beans. How much do you think one cup is?* Record children's responses on chart paper.

6 Show the class the 1-cup measure. *How many handfuls of beans do you think will fit in this cup?* Have children make a pile in front of them that they think equals one cup, and then distribute a 1-cup measure to each pair to check their estimates. *Can we use handfuls when we're following a recipe? Why or why not?*

Today children compare the 1-cup measuring cup with the class's container collection. They will sort four containers by capacity and discover some interesting facts along the way.

1 Discuss children's past experiences with liquid measure. *What are some liquids we use that are measured? Looking at our collection of containers might give us some ideas.* Write children's ideas on chart paper. *Why do you think such liquids need to be measured? How is measurement used in cooking?*

> milk
>
> juice
>
> cough syrup
>
> gasoline
>
> soft drinks
>
> maple syrup
>
> water in our houses

2 *Is it a problem if the chef uses too much or too little of an ingredient?* The discussion is likely to bring out children's experiences with standard measuring cups at home. Remind the class of the activity in Setting Out, discussing the usefulness of the plastic 1-cup measuring cup for a standard measure.

3 Show the class the three coffee cups you've brought in. *Could the chef use any of these to measure one cup?* The discussion should identify the fact that the cups do not hold the same amount. The children may decide they need to fill the cups to determine whether they hold exactly the same amount as a cup.

4 Have each pair choose four small containers from the class collection. *Look at the cups all around you.*

- *How are they alike? How are some of them different?*

- *Do all of these containers have the same capacity? How do you know?*

- *Are any of them 1-cup measures?*

- *Which hold more than a cup?*

- *Which hold less than a cup?*

Because they have not yet had the collection of understandings necessary to conserve volume, children at this age may think the taller containers will hold more and will be surprised at their findings. This activity provides opportunities for children to think about ideas related to measuring volume.

MathLand® Smart Strands • Grades K–2
© Creative Publications

5 *Today I'd like you to work with your partner. Put the containers in two groups: "more than 1 cup" and "less than 1 cup." Make a drawing of the two groups.*

Deciding that a container holds about one cup, or a little more than a cup, requires thinking and discussion between partners. Allow the children to complete the measuring and ordering for themselves. It is the process of thinking that is important for children at this point, not making perfect measurements.

Less than
1 cup

More than
1 cup

6 *How can you check your guesses?* Let children use the beans and measuring cups to investigate the capacity of the containers.

7 At the end of math time, bring the class together to discuss the project.

- *Did anything surprise you when you checked your sorting? What was it?*

- *Do you think you get better at making estimates as you do it more? Tell us how.*

Math Journal

Have students write a few sentences telling what they found out when putting the containers in order.

Home Work

At home this week, have children find three different containers that hold close to one cup. Suggest children use water in the sink or bathtub to measure. Have them sketch the containers, label each sketch "exactly 1 cup," "more than 1 cup," or "less than 1 cup."

We've measured the capacity in cups of many containers. Now we focus on other measures of capacity and how they are related.

1 Have all the containers distributed to groups of children. *You've been using a cup as your unit of measure. There are other units for measuring capacity. Some of them are named on the containers.* Display a chart like the one shown. *Can you find a pint in your collection? A quart?* Allow time for children to look at the containers and find examples. *Does your pint look like my pint?*

ounce

pint

quart

half-gallon

gallon

liter

2 Set one each of the following containers where the whole class can see them: half-pint or cup, pint, quart, half-gallon, gallon, liter. Discuss their names. *What have you seen these containers used for? Why do you think they make them in those sizes?*

| Celia: | If the milk container was bigger than a gallon, it would be hard to pick up. |
| Danny: | If it was smaller than the small milk carton, it would be too small. |

The metric measurement system makes the liter the standard unit of capacity. This system was first adopted in France and is in general use in most of the countries in the world. It is universally used for scientific measurements. Most English-speaking countries, however, use what the U.S. calls the customary system of measurement, which utilizes cups, pints, quarts, and gallons to measure capacity.

3 Hold up the pint container. Write the word *estimate* on the board. *How many cups do you think will fit in a pint?* Write some estimates on the board.

4 *How could you be sure your estimates were right?* After taking suggestions, model how to measure two cups of beans carefully into the pint jar.

| $\frac{1}{2}$ pint | pint | quart | $\frac{1}{2}$ gallon | gallon | liter |

5 Distribute How Many Cups? (page 100) to each child and go over the chart. Show children how they can already fill in "2 cups" for "1 pint," as well as their estimates.

6 Have children write in estimates for each of the containers. Then distribute the containers, one per group, so groups can use the measuring cup and beans to measure the actual amounts. ***How can we be sure that we're measuring carefully? How can you work together with your group to do your best work?***

Name _____

How Many Cups?

Container	Estimate	Actual
Half-Pint		
Pint		
Quart		
Half-Gallon		
Gallon		
Liter		

7 At the end of math time, have pairs present their findings to the class. Write on chart paper the relationships they report, and allow time for children to fill in their personal charts.

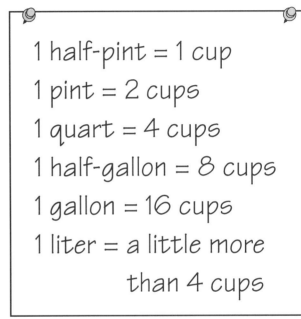

1 half-pint = 1 cup
1 pint = 2 cups
1 quart = 4 cups
1 half-gallon = 8 cups
1 gallon = 16 cups
1 liter = a little more
        than 4 cups

8 *Does anyone notice anything about his chart? How is the liter different from the other containers? Here's a challenge: How many pints are in a quart? How many quarts are in a gallon?*

Interview Assessment

As the children are working, approach individuals and ask, *Tell me how you estimate how much a container will hold. Are you surprised about any of your containers?*

It's About Time

This week we learn about different aspects of time. We begin with a discussion about a single day, then begin to build an understanding of calendars, mapping the days of the week, months, and a year. After learning about the months in our calendar, we take a look at the Mayan calendar to see how another culture organizes time.

Key Mathematical Ideas

★ There are 7 days in a week, and 365 days or 12 months in a year.

★ Calendars have a particular order that helps us organize time.

★ Dates and schedules are important for many reasons.

Prior Knowledge

Since a child's understanding of time develops slowly, it is important to revisit and expand upon these activities throughout the year. While children progress from smaller to larger units of time on each of the following day trips, the activities do not necessarily have to happen in the order presented or on consecutive days.

WHAT THE CHILDREN WILL DO

• Describe and sequence a day's events
• Chart the class's weekly schedule
• Develop an accurate month calendar
• Examine the structure of our calendar system

Getting Ready

Materials

• chart paper

• 5" × 8" index cards, 6 for each child

• 4–5 sentence strips (or large index cards), for each group

• paper plates or index cards

• adding machine tape

Preparation

 • For Day Trip Three, write the numbers of the days of the current month on a strip of adding machine tape. For Day Trip Four, bring two old calendars to class. Cut the months of one calendar into "puzzle pieces," cutting off any squares without dates in them. Write the month on the back of each piece. For Day Trip Five, make copies of Mayan Calendar Symbols (page 101), one for each child.

We start our week on time discussing what happens in one day. We make zigzag books telling about our favorite way to spend a day.

1 To get children thinking about a day as a unit of time, invite the class to think about activities they could do in one day as well as things that would be impossible to do in one day. *How are you deciding which activities you can do in one day? Does it take more than a day or less than a day to do this activity?*

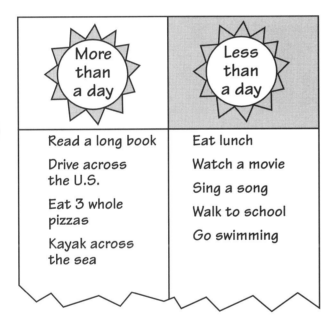

More than a day	Less than a day
Read a long book	Eat lunch
Drive across the U.S.	Watch a movie
Eat 3 whole pizzas	Sing a song
Kayak across the sea	Walk to school
	Go swimming

2 Ask the children to think about the activities that regularly happen in a day. On chart paper start making a list of things children do every day: wake up, brush their teeth, eat breakfast, and so on. *Which activities usually take place in the morning? afternoon? evening?*

3 *You are going to create a favorite day.* Decide on certain things that everyone will do, such as wake up, eat three meals, and sleep. Emphasize to the class the sequencing of events. Tape the index cards, accordion-style, to make zigzag books. Each child should draw pictures and write (or dictate) sentences to show what she would do during her day. Remind the children to plan what they will show on each page before drawing and writing.

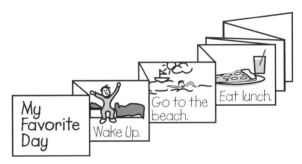

4 Make an exhibit of the zigzag books, encouraging children to read each other's books during math and reading time. Later, come together to share observations about favorite days. *Did several people visit the same place or do the same thing? Were our favorite days busier or less busy than average days?*

There is a variety of ways to connect writing to math activities. Depending on your class, this activity might work well with younger children pairing up and dictating ideas to older children.

Today we're going to learn about the days of the week. We'll make a weekly schedule showing the activities we do each day in school.

1 Begin with a discussion about the days in a week. *What day is today? Who knows what day it was yesterday? What day will it be tomorrow? How many days are in one week? Let's see if we can list all of the days of the week in order.* Write the days on sentence strips. Shuffle the cards a few times and see if pairs or groups of children can line them up in order.

2 *Let's make a calendar showing some of the things you do at school. Which days are we in school?* Display the weekday name cards on a bulletin board.

3 As a whole class, label the things that happen every day, such as recess, lunch, math time, and so on. Then divide the class into groups and have each group illustrate activities that happen on a specific day of the week. Children can work from memory and then consult with you to be sure they have included all of the day's activities. Paper plates or large index cards work well for the illustrations.

4 As children finish their drawings, invite them to attach the drawings to the bulletin board. Have them state the day of the activity and whether it occurs in the morning or afternoon (older children could add the time).

5 When the board is assembled, come together to discuss the schedule. *Who can find the picture showing what we do after snack on Tuesday? Who sees something we do every day in the afternoon?*

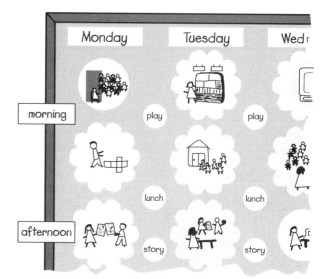

6 Use this opportunity to have a broader conversation about schedules. *What do we use a schedule for? If a visitor came to our class and saw this bulletin board, what would he learn? What other places have schedules? Why?*

There is an abundance of literature about time for primary-age children. Children will enjoy listening to poetry and stories about days of the week, months, and seasons. You might have a class scavenger hunt to gather a collection of books about time.

Children will construct their own calendars of the current month.

1 Discuss with the class why people use calendars. Then invite the class to make a month calendar, using everything they know about calendars. This task can help you determine their prior knowledge of calendars as well as help assess what children have learned by the end of the week. When children have finished have them share their work. Use their contributions to make a bulletin board or chart titled *What We Already Know About Calendars.*

2 Show the class the adding-machine tape you have prepared numbering the days of the month. **This shows the number of days in this month. Does this seem like a good way to make a calendar?** Have a calendar available for children to look at the organization and make comparisons.

3 Invite children to come up and cut your number line to make a traditional calendar. Before children cut the number line, have them explain to the class why they want to cut it in a certain place.

Laura	We should cut the number line at the two because that's Saturday. Sunday is May third.
Mikiko	Now we cut the line after every seven numbers.

4 Paste your number line calendar on chart paper, labeling the days of the week, holidays, and so on. Make a collage or group picture showing something special about the month. Engage the children in conversation about the calendar. *If we have P. E. on Mondays, how many times will we have P. E. this month? How would you say this date?* (point to a number on the calendar)

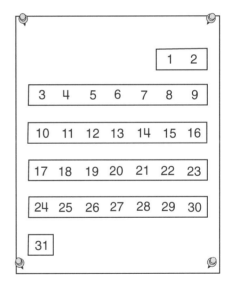

Home Work

Have children collect papers with the date stamped or written on them. Items can include envelopes, appointment cards, checks, tickets, and newspapers.

The idea of a month beginning and ending in the middle of the week can be confusing. To help children get a better grasp of this concept, we make calendar puzzles from old calendars.

1 As a group, browse through a calendar. Notice the different features. *How many months are there? How many days? Why do you think the people who made this calendar decided to put this picture in August?* List all of the months in order on the board. Discuss which months children are in school, which months are vacation, which months are winter, and so on.

2 Look through the calendar again, this time asking children to point out the days of the week where different months begin and end. *Why are all these squares at the beginning of May blank? If we turn back to April, what should we find? Can someone explain why every month cannot begin on Sunday?*

3 Take out the calendar that has been cut into month pieces. *We want to organize these 12 months into a whole year. What should we do first?* With the children directing and determining the steps, line up the months to show a year fitting together like one long puzzle. At the top of the puzzle, list the days of the week in large, bold letters.

Interview Assessment

Open a calendar and ask, *How many days are in this month? What date is the second Tuesday? If today is the third of the month, how many days until the eleventh?*

---

4 Once you have your calendar puzzle assembled, gather the children around it. Share observations. *What interesting things do you notice? Then ask questions like these: Find the last day of February. What day is it? So that means March 1st will fall on what day? If one month ends on a Monday, when will the following month start? Let's look at our calendar puzzle to find out.* Children can come up with their own calendar challenges to pose to the class.

S	M	T	W	Th	F	S
1	2	3	4	5	6	7
8	9	10	11	12	13	14
15	16	17	18	19	20	21
22	23	24	25	26	27	28
29	1	2	3	4	5	6
7	8	9	10	11	12	13
14	15	16	17	18	19	20
21	22	23	24	25	26	27
28	29	30	31	1	2	3
4	5	6	7	8	9	10
11	12	13	14	15	16	17
18	19	20	21	22	23	24
25	26	27	28	29	30	1
2	3	4	5	6	7	8
9	10	11	12	13	14	15
16	17	18	19	20	21	22
23	24	25	26	27	28	29
30	31					

5 You might want to include some challenging questions for children to think about and solve during the next few days. *Where is the middle of the year? How many days from Independence Day to Halloween?*

MathLand® Smart Strands • Grades K–2
© Creative Publications

Today we'll take a look at a calendar from another culture. We'll find some similarities and differences between our calendar and the Mayan calendar.

1 *Today we are going to look at a different calendar. We're going to see how the Maya have tracked time for hundreds of years in Central America and Mexico.*

2 *The Mayan haab calendar has 365 days. It has months, days, and dates like our calendar. The haab calendar has 18 months plus 5 extra days. Each month has 20 specific day names. The Maya identify each month and day with a picture as well as a name.* Distribute the Mayan Calendar Symbols (page 101) and invite children to discuss the names and pictures.

3 Have children work in pairs to find similarities and differences between the haab calendar and the calendar we use. Then bring the class together to create a chart like the one shown.

Same	Different
Both have 365 days in a year. Both have years, months, and days. Both have names for days and months.	Mayan calendar uses pictures to name months and days. Mayan calendar has 20 day names, ours has only 7. Mayan calendar has 18 months, ours has only 12.

4 *The Maya thought that the symbol of the day you were born on was significant. For instance,* **Imix** *means crocodile. What do you think it might mean if you were born on that day?* Children might enjoy painting their favorite symbol on construction paper to display in the classroom.

The Mayan 260-day ritual, or *tzolkin,* calendar is represented by a sequence of numbers from 1 to 13. These numbers cycle with another sequence of 20 days, each day with its own name and symbol. The Maya combined this tzolkin calendar with the 365-day solar calendar, or *haab,* to create a cycle of 52 years. The calendar is still in use today. You can learn more about the Mayan calendar by looking in encyclopedias and books.

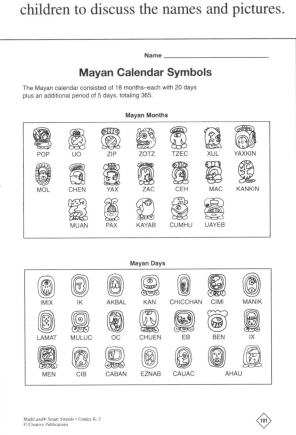

Name _____

Mayan Calendar Symbols

The Mayan calendar consisted of 18 months–each with 20 days plus an additional period of 5 days, totaling 365.

Mayan Months

POP, UO, ZIP, ZOTZ, TZEC, XUL, YAXKIN

MOL, CHEN, YAX, ZAC, CEH, MAC, KANKIN

MUAN, PAX, KAYAB, CUMHU, UAYEB

Mayan Days

IMIX, IK, AKBAL, KAN, CHICCHAN, CIMI, MANIK

LAMAT, MULUC, OC, CHUEN, EB, BEN, IX

MEN, CIB, CABAN, EZNAB, CAUAC, AHAU

MathLand® Smart Strands • Grades K–2
© Creative Publications

101

Order in Our World

This week we learn how patterns and classification systems are a part of our everyday life. We explore patterns in odd and even numbers and create our own rules to sort objects.

Key Mathematical Ideas

★ There are patterns in cause-and-effect relationships.

★ Patterns and classification systems are found in our environment.

★ Rules can be made to sort items by their attributes.

★ Items can be sorted by more than one attribute.

Prior Knowledge

The children should have experience making and identifying patterns as well as grouping and sorting objects. They should be able to count to 20. The children should be able to work in pairs.

WHAT THE CHILDREN WILL DO

• Play a cause-and-effect matching game

• Identify patterns

• Make up a sorting rule to sort animal cards

• Classify food in *Today Is Monday* by Eric Carle

Getting Ready

Materials

• LinkerCubes, 20 per pair

• full sheets of paper

• quarter sheets of paper

• chart paper

• 3" × 5" index cards, 6 per child

• tape

• scissors

• Overhead LinkerCubes

Preparation

 • For Day Trip Four, cut enough yarn to make a large ring. Cut four-foot pieces of yarn, one for each pair. Gather old magazines or calendars with animal pictures. For Day Trip Five, get Eric Carle's *Today Is Monday,* published by Philomel Books, 1993.

Red light—stop. Green light—go. Today we'll make predictions about cause-and-effect relationships. Then we'll have fun playing a matching game.

1 *Let's play a game. I'll say something, then you say what you think might come next. For example, if I say, "The traffic light turns red," you might say, "The cars will stop."*

2 Play the game with the class. As you say a "cause," write it on chart paper. Then when a child responds, write the corresponding "effect" next to it. As the children become more comfortable with this concept, give them a chance to name "causes" as well.

Cause	Effect
red traffic light	cars stop
green traffic light	cars go
rain	umbrellas go up
fire alarm goes off	firefighters come
turn on radio	sound comes out
turn on oven	oven heats up
time for bed	brush your teeth or get into your pajamas
lunch time	eat food

During the game, the children may come up with more than one effect that matches a cause. Not all situations have just one effect. Encourage the children to talk about whether they think this is true or not.

3 *Now let's think up our own cause-and-effect situations.* Pass out six index cards to each child. *On one index card, draw a "cause" picture. On another index card, draw the "effect." Draw three situations that show cause and effect.*

4 When the children are done, have them take their cards and sit in groups of three. *Now we're going to play a matching game.* Go over the rules with the children, then let them play. If time permits, have the groups rotate to a new set of cards so they can see more cause-and-effect situations.

How to Play Cause and Effect

1. Place the cards face down.

2. Take turns flipping over two cards at a time.

3. If the cards make a cause-and-effect situation, keep the cards and flip two more cards over.

4. If the cards don't make a cause-and-effect situation, turn the cards back over.

5. Continue playing until all possible matches are made.

Interview Assessment

As the children make their cards, approach a child and say, *Tell me about your favorite cause-and-effect situation.*

Day Trip Two
PATTERN DETECTIVES

This Day Trip takes us outside the classroom. We put on our sleuthing caps as we hunt for patterns. Look what we discover! There are patterns all around us.

1 *Today we're going to be detectives— pattern detectives. We're going to look for patterns around us. Can someone give me an example of a pattern?* Review several examples of patterns with the class to make sure everyone has an understanding of the concept.

2 *Let's start our detective work!* Take a walk outside or through the hallways. Have the children take paper, pencils, and a hard surface on which to write. Write down the patterns you find.

3 Back in the classroom discuss what types of patterns the children found. *Where did you see a pattern? Describe the pattern.*

> *What patterns did you see?*
>
> **Mikiko** In the parking lot, there are lines for cars. I saw this pattern, space-line, space-line.
>
> **Kalil** I did too. I called it ABAB.

Some children will be more advanced than others at translating or expressing their patterns using letters, colors, or numbers. Encourage those who are able, to create, extend, and translate patterns.

4 Hand out sheets of paper. *Draw a picture that shows a pattern you found.* Give the children time to draw their patterns.

5 *Now let's use another sheet of paper to hide all but a piece of our pattern.* Demonstrate how to tape another sheet of paper over the pattern, leaving only a portion of the pattern exposed.

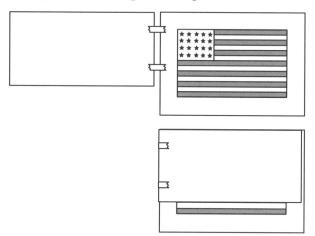

6 When the children are done taping, have them exchange papers with a partner. *Where did the pattern come from? What will the picture inside show? What comes next in the pattern?* The children can guess the pattern and then check by lifting the flap. Put the finished pictures in a box at a learning center with the title "Our Outdoor Patterns."

Math Journal

Students can draw patterns in their journals and name them in different ways, such as with numbers or letters.

MathLand® Smart Strands • Grades K–2
© Creative Publications

Our look at patterns continues. Today we find another pattern—odd and even numbers. How are they different?

1 *What is a pair? How many items are in a pair?* Spend a few minutes talking about items that come in pairs. The children might mention shoes, mittens, or eyes. Determine as a class that items in pairs come in twos.

2 *Let's use our LinkerCubes to represent numbers. Start with one. Represent it with LinkerCubes. Can you make a pair? Draw what you see.* Model the first three numbers with the class on the overhead projector.

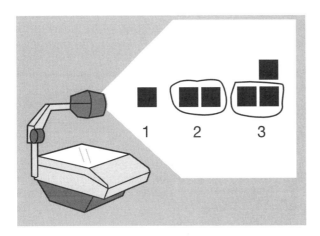

3 Then have the children work in pairs, representing all the numbers one through ten. The children should identify the pairs in each number by putting LinkerCubes together in groups of two.

4 When the children are done, gather the class for a discussion. On the chalkboard, list the numbers one through ten in a row. *Did some of the numbers have extra LinkerCubes that didn't make a pair? Which numbers were they?* Underline those numbers. *Which numbers broke into pairs with no extras?* Circle those numbers. *Can you see a pattern? Describe the pattern.*

5 *Mathematicians call numbers without extras* even numbers. *They call numbers with extras* odd numbers.

All numbers that are divisible by two are even numbers. If a number is not divisible by two, it is an odd number.

6 *Now work with your partner. Can you find all the even and odd numbers through 20?* Let the pairs work using LinkerCubes if needed.

7 Bring the children together to discuss what they found.

- *What are the even numbers through 20?*

- *What are the odd numbers through 20?*

- *How did you know?*

- *What patterns did you notice?*

- *Do you think this pattern continues past 20?*

Day Trip Four
ANIMAL ATTRIBUTES

Today we play a sorting game with our partners. Can we sort our animal cards according to the rule?

1 Pass out old magazines and four or more quarter sheets of paper to each child. *Today we're going to play a game, but first we need to make the cards for our game. Find and cut out pictures of animals. Paste one animal on each sheet of paper.*

Some children will find animals that may not fit on the quarter sheet. Encourage those children to paste a portion of the animal so that someone can recognize it.

2 Gather the class together. *Look at your animals. What are some things you notice about them? These are called* **attributes.** Write on chart paper the attributes of the animals as the children suggest them.

Animal Attributes

- four legs
- two legs
- wings
- fur
- feathers
- brown
- beak
- claws
- scales

3 Have the children bring their animal cards and sit in a circle. Form a ring in the center with yarn. *Let's play a game. Suppose I picked a sorting rule, such as "has four legs." What animals could go in our ring?* Go around the circle, having the children place one of their animal pictures either inside the ring if it meets the sorting rule or outside the ring if it does not meet the rule. Model the game a few more times.

4 Then have pairs use their animal cards to play the game. They can draw a ring on a large sheet of paper or use yarn. One child makes up a sorting rule, then they each take turns sorting their animal cards according to the rule. Pairs take turns making up sorting rules.

As a challenge for more advanced children, ask them to think of a rule using two attributes, for example, "has four legs" and "is brown."

5 Near the end of math time, have the children play one more sorting game and then draw a picture to tell about it. Afterwards let pairs share their recordings.

- *How did you sort your animal cards in this game? What was your rule?*

- *How did you decide what to put inside the ring? Outside the ring?*

- *Would a [animal] belong inside the ring or outside the ring in this game? Why?*

MathLand® Smart Strands • Grades K–2
© Creative Publications

How are foods grouped in the supermarket? Today we take a look and begin to understand that things are grouped, or classified, in a logical way.

Encourage dialog to help identify similarities and differences among classification strategies. Classification encourages clear and logical thinking. It is fundamental to learning about the physical world. If time permits, plan a class trip to a supermarket for a first-hand look at its classification system.

1 Read Eric Carle's book, *Today Is Monday.* Discuss the story and ask the class to recall the foods in the correct order. You may wish to sing the song at the end of the book. *Suppose we had to buy these items at the supermarket. Where would we find them? First let's list some of the different sections in a market.* Record the children's responses on chart paper.

Supermarket Sections

- frozen foods
- milk and yogurt
- fruit
- vegetables
- cereal
- pasta
- cookies
- crackers
- soap
- chips
- drinks

2 *When we want to keep things organized, we sometimes group them in a certain way. This list shows how some things are grouped in a supermarket. This is called classifying. How can we classify the foods in Eric Carle's story? What kind of string beans are served to the porcupine?* Explain that sometimes a food can be found in different places depending on whether it's fresh, frozen, or in a can.

3 Group the children into pairs. *Draw a map of a supermarket. Label the sections on your map, such as milk and eggs. Then write the foods from* **Today Is Monday** *in the section where they should go.* (Less advanced children can draw pictures.) If there is time, name other items for the children to classify.

4 Post the maps on a bulletin board, then discuss them with the class.

- *How are the maps alike?*
- *How are they different?*
- *What are the different sections?*
- *Did you find sections for all the food in the story? Why or why not?*
- *How does grouping, or classifying, objects help us?*

Home Work Have the children look for classification systems in their own homes, such as a silverware drawer, kitchen cupboard, or closet. Each child can share one classification discovery from home.

Pairs and Pairs

Patterns are everywhere. This week we take a look at number patterns—how sets of numbers relate. We develop an idea of a functional relationship by observing the regularity between pairs of numbers in the charts we create and the games we play. Our work this week helps us see mathematical relationships and prepares us for abstract thinking in the years ahead.

WHAT THE CHILDREN WILL DO

- Identify number patterns in charts
- Write problems related to the charts
- Play Number Machine and determine the rule, or pattern, for the game

Key Mathematical Ideas

★ Patterns can be found in a list of related number pairs.

★ By identifying a pattern, a list of related number pairs can be extended.

★ Real-world problems can be solved using patterns found in a list of related number pairs.

★ The generalization of numerical patterns provides a background for work with functions.

Prior Knowledge

The children should be able to count to 100, and they should be able to identify and describe a number pattern.

Getting Ready

Materials

- 1 set of Pattern Blocks for each pair
- chart paper
- full sheets of paper for each pair
- scissors
- Overhead Pattern Blocks

Preparation

 • For Day Trip One, copy Bike Orders (page 102), one order per child. Cut apart the orders. For Day Trip Five, copy Number Machine (page 103), one per child. If you wish, make the number machine books ahead of time. Copy the Number Machine game rules on chart paper.

The bicycle orders are streaming in! How many wheels do we need to fill an order? Today we write order forms for the number of wheels we need.

1 *Today the owner of the Rolling Racer Bike factory has put us in charge. We have to figure out how many wheels to order to meet the latest orders for bicycles.*

2 *Here's an order for three bicycles. How many wheels do we need to make three bicycles? Talk with your partner and try to come up with a way to solve this problem.* After the children have had time to work, ask some of them to explain their thinking.

> The children will probably have different solutions. Some will count by ones, others by twos. Some children may draw a picture and count the number of wheels. All children will gain by hearing that there are many strategies for solving problems of this type.

3 *Now let's write an order form for the number of wheels we need.* On the overhead projector, show the children how to write an order form.

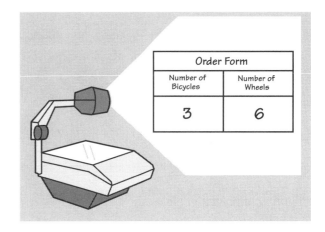

Order Form	
Number of Bicycles	Number of Wheels
3	6

4 *The orders for bicycles are piling up! Everyone must take an order so we can catch up.* Pass out a bicycle order to each child. *Make a wheel order form showing how many wheels you need to make the number of bicycles on your order.*

5 After the children are done, gather the class and talk about their orders.

- *How did you figure out how many wheels you needed to order?*

- *Did anyone figure it out a different way? How?*

- *What if you were filling an order for tricycles? How would you figure out how many wheels to order?*

Ordering will be easy once we make our bicycle wheel chart. We can look up the number of bikes ordered to find the number of wheels we need. Can we make a chart for tricycle orders, too?

1 *Yesterday we figured out how many wheels we needed for each bicycle order. We had several orders for the same number of bicycles. How could we save time figuring out the number of wheels we need?* Listen to the children's suggestions. If the children don't suggest making a chart, propose the idea yourself.

2 *What would our bicycle wheel chart look like? What information do we need to show?* Draw the start of the chart on the overhead projector.

3 *If we got an order for one bicycle, how many wheels would we need to order? Two bicycles? Three bicycles?* Fill in the chart as the children respond. Explain how to read the chart each time.

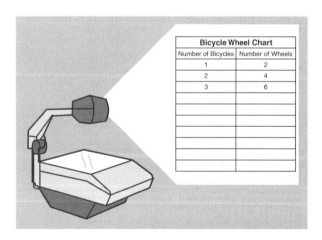

Bicycle Wheel Chart

Number of Bicycles	Number of Wheels
1	2
2	4
3	6

4 *Do you notice any patterns in our chart?* Continue filling in the chart if needed.

Do you see a pattern?	
Awenita	The number of wheels increases by two each time.
Danny	I just doubled the number of bicycles to find the number of wheels.

5 *How many wheels would we need for ten bicycles? How do you know?* Finish the chart through ten bicycles. *Now that we've made this chart we can easily find the number of wheels we need for our orders.*

6 *Uh, oh! Orders for tricycles are coming in. We need a tricycle wheel chart to help us determine the number of wheels we need.* Have children make a tricycle wheel chart showing orders for one to ten tricycles. (Tricycles have one large front wheel and two small rear wheels. Children may or may not make this distinction in their charts.)

7 After the children are done, talk about their tricycle wheel charts.

- *How many wheels do you need for four tricycles? How do you know?*

- *How did you figure out how to make your chart?*

- *What patterns can you find?*

- *How would you find how many wheels you would need for 20 tricycles?*

MathLand® Smart Strands • Grades K–2
© Creative Publications

In this Day Trip, we make tile designs and create tile charts showing the number of tiles to order. Now we're ready for the orders to start!

1 *Today we're going to be tile designers for Tile Town Designs. Let's make a tile design.* On the overhead projector, make a simple design using two types of Pattern Blocks. Show several more simple designs.

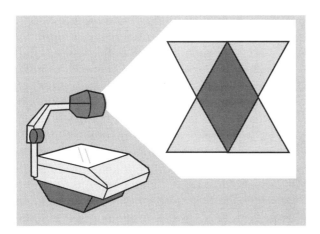

2 *Suppose we wanted to make two of these designs. How many Pattern Blocks of each color would we need? What about three designs?* Start a chart showing the number of tiles needed.

3 Have the children work in pairs with Pattern Blocks to create their own tile designs using 5 Pattern Blocks. The children can draw their tile design by tracing the Pattern Blocks and coloring them in.

4 *How many of each kind of tile will it take to make one of your designs? Two designs? Make a tile design chart showing the number of tiles you need to make from one to ten designs.*

5 At the end of math time, have the children share their designs and charts.

- *Tell about your design. How many of each Pattern Block did you use?*

- *How did you figure out how to make your tile design chart?*

- *What patterns do you see?*

- *How would you figure out how many tiles you would need for more than ten designs?*

- *What design would you make next time? Why?*

Interview Assessment

As you observe the children creating their charts, ask, *What number will come next? How do you know?* Note whether the children are skip counting or whether they start counting by ones each time.

This Day Trip will take us to the kooky critters assembly line. We draw a plan for a kooky critter and create a parts chart for kooky critter assemblers to follow.

1 *Today we'll be working on a kooky critter assembly line. We'll get to create our own kooky critters.* Explain that one kooky critter can have ten or fewer parts. *Let's make a kooky critter and start a parts chart.*

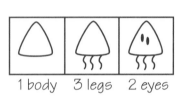

1 body   3 legs   2 eyes

2 Fill in the chart with the children, showing the number of parts for up to five kooky critters. Explain how to read the chart as you complete it.

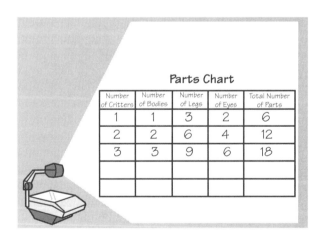

Parts Chart

Number of Critters	Number of Bodies	Number of Legs	Number of Eyes	Total Number of Parts
1	1	3	2	6
2	2	6	4	12
3	3	9	6	18

3 Ask questions about the chart.

- *Suppose we used nine legs. How many bodies did we use? How do you know?*

- *Suppose we used a total of 24 parts. How many kooky critters did we make?*

- *Suppose we used two bodies. How many legs did we use?*

- *Can you predict how many eyes you would need to make six kooky critters? Explain your thinking.*

- *What patterns do you see?*

4 *Now it's time to make your own kooky critters and parts chart.* Have the children work with a partner to complete the task.

5 When the children are done, have them write problems for others to solve. Put the problems, kooky critters, and part charts on a bulletin board. The children can solve the problems in their free time.

Home Work

At home, have the children create a parts chart for a piece of furniture, for example, one chair, two arms, four legs, one body, seven total parts. The children can show how many parts are needed for up to five pieces of furniture.

Today we play Number Machine. We put a number in the machine and watch what comes out. Can we predict what will appear?

1 Draw a box and an In/Out chart on the overhead projector. *I have a special number machine. If I put in the number 2, out comes the number 4.* Show a 2 going in the machine and a 4 coming out. Write the number 2 in the In column and 4 in the Out column.

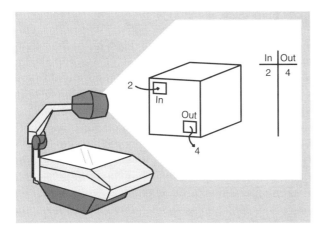

2 *If I put in the number 3, out comes the number 6. Now I'm going to put in the number 4. Can you predict what number will come out? Why do you think that?* Continue putting numbers in until someone guesses what number comes out.

3 Play several games with the class. Ask the children to explain their thinking each time.

Use mathematical ideas the children have recently encountered. These could include multiples, adding ten to each number, or doubling each number. Be sure to put in zero each time. Children will start to recognize that zero often reveals interesting twists to the rules.

4 Have the children use the Number Machine reproducible to create number machine books. Staple the books at the top of the pages. Once they've made the books, the children can play Number Machine in pairs. Review the rules with the class.

How to Play Number Machine

1. The game has a Rule Master and a Guesser.

2. The Rule Master makes up a rule. (For example, 7 becomes 70. The rule is "Put a zero on the end of the number.")

3. The Rule Master writes the rule in her book, then folds under the rule so it can't be seen. She puts an example in the chart.

4. The Guesser asks, "What does [number] turn into?"

5. The Rule Master runs the number through the machine, records it on her chart, then tells and records the answer.

6. The Guesser records the number and the answer in his book and tries to guess the rule.

7. The game ends when the Guesser says the rule. Then players change roles and play again.

Let's Find Out

How did you get to school today? How many people are in your family? The questions we ask this week help us learn more about our classmates and show us how we are alike and different. We find that the answers to some questions don't change from day to day, while others may. Throughout the week, the graphs we make together help us see our information more clearly.

Key Mathematical Ideas

★ Each person has characteristics that are like and different from the characteristics of others.

★ Data can be presented in graphs using pictures and symbols.

★ One-to-one correspondence helps determine relative sizes of groups of objects.

Prior Knowledge

Students should be able to count to 20 and to understand the concept of one-to-one correspondence.

WHAT THE CHILDREN WILL DO

• Answer questions about themselves

• Make class picture graphs

• Use data from a graph to comment on what they have in common with classmates

Getting Ready

Materials

• quarter sheets of paper

• half sheets of paper

• colored construction paper

• chart paper

• scissors

• clipboards

Preparation

• Prepare this week's graph formats. For a more durable classroom graphing mat, use a light colored shower curtain or liner. Draw the graph format on with permanent marker. For Looking Back, cut out multiple copies of a child-size hand, one per child plus a few extras (optional).

How are we alike and different? We find out a lot about each other today as we stand in groups to show our answers to a number of interesting questions.

1 Gather the children in a group on the rug. *This week I'll be asking you lots of questions about yourselves. We'll find out how we're alike and different.* Ask the children to look around at their classmates and think of what they know about them or can tell by looking. Call on volunteers to suggest things that some of the children in the class have in common. *How are some of us alike?*

2 For each suggestion (long hair, for example), have the children who fit the characteristic stand up. *Which group is bigger, the people with long hair* (those who are standing) *or the people who don't have long hair* (the people sitting)? *Is there anyone who is sitting who you think should be standing? Why? What if we asked this question again at the end of the school year? Would everyone still be in the same group? What if nobody in our class got their hair cut for a year? What would happen? How would our standing and sitting groups be different?*

3 Continue with standing and sitting groups in response to several more of the children's suggestions. In each case, it may be interesting to see whether the children can identify the group with the greatest number of members just by eyeballing the groups. In cases where the groups are of similar size, ask the groups to line up side by side. Have group members extend their arms or hold hands with the corresponding person from the other group. This will help the children determine, by one-to-one correspondence, which group is largest.

All of the comparison work today may be done without actually counting the number of people in the groups. In many cases, children will be able to comment about which group is larger or smaller based solely on visual assessment. In the cases where you line the groups up next to each other, the larger group's "leftovers" (those children without a partner in the other line) will be the clue that that group includes more members.

4 Tell the children that tomorrow you will have some different questions to ask them about themselves. *Tomorrow we'll try a different way to show our groups.*

Home Work At home this week, have the children ask questions of family members to find out how they are alike and different. *Are you older than seven? Do you like* [name of a food]? *Do you like* [name of a holiday]? *Is there red in your clothing?*

What color is your hair? How did you get to school? We make graphs with pictures to show our answers to a variety of questions about ourselves. During the week, we find that we have something in common with almost everyone in our class.

1 Tell the children that they will be sharing information about themselves and showing it in a special format called a *graph*. Show the class the chart paper or shower curtain graph format you have prepared. Tell them that you will ask them a new question each day and then will help them organize their answers on the graph.

2 Each day select a question from the list shown. Pose the question, then have the children answer by drawing pictures to place on the graph.

Graphing Questions

- *How did you get to school today?*
  Have the children make small pictures of cars, buses, bikes, or feet to place on the graph. The children should put their names on their drawings.
- *What color is your hair?*
  The children can draw pictures of themselves to show their hair color. Remind them to include their names on their drawings.
- *Are you wearing long pants, shorts, or a dress/skirt today?*
  Ask the children to draw pants, shorts, or skirts to place on the graph.

3 Help the group organize their drawings into a graph. Use folded note cards with pictures or symbols to label each column. One at a time, have each child place his or her drawing in the appropriate graph column.

It will be a challenge for many children this age to glean information from the class graphs. Model by using a "thinking to yourself" voice to comment about the graph in progress. For example, voicing thoughts like, *Hmmm, it looks as if a lot of people have brown hair.* Or *Robbie is like me. We both have on long pants today.* Vocalizing your thoughts will help the children begin to articulate their own thoughts.

4 When the day's graph is complete, ask the children to make comments about what the graph shows.

- *Which way of getting to school is the most popular?*

- *How many children get to school the same way you do?*

- *Which column has the fewest pictures in it?*

- *If I asked this question yesterday, would you have marked the same answer?*

- *Would this pants, shorts, and skirts graph look the same if we graphed it every day for a week? Why?*

Side Trip

Surveys

Suggest to the children that they conduct surveys to find out more about their classmates. The children may generate their own questions, or you may pose a few from which they can choose. During free time, interested children may go around the classroom with clipboards and pencils, asking their question of classmates and drawing pictures or writing *yes* or *no* to record the answers. Here are some sample survey questions:

- Do you have a pet?

- What's your favorite color?

- Would you like to be in my play of Snow White?

- Do you want to play jump rope with me at recess?

- What's your favorite book?

- Have you ever been stung by a bee?

Interview Assessment

Have a child look at the class's graph from that day and ask, *What does this graph show us?*

How many people in your family? We make an interesting graph, then draw pictures of our families to share on the bulletin board.

1 *We've found out a lot about each other during the last couple of days. Today I have one more question for you.* Ask the children how many people are in their family, including themselves. Show them the hand shape you have cut out, and demonstrate how to fold down the fingers to show certain numbers.

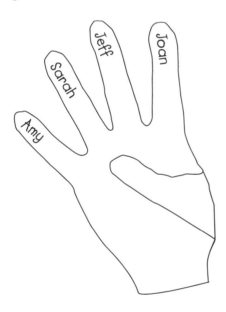

2 Have each child trace her hand and cut out the shape. She should fold down the fingers so that the hand shows the number of people in her family. (Some children may need two hands to represent the people in their families.) Remind the children to write their names on their cutouts. Some children may know how to write the names of their family members. If they wish, they may write the name of each person in their family on one of the fingers of their hand cutouts.

3 Help the children place their cutouts on a graph. As the graph takes shape, talk about what it shows.

- *Who else has the same number of people in his family as you do?*

- *Can you name someone with more people in her family than you have?*

- *Look! Right now the graph has the same number of three- and four-person families.*

- *What if we counted pets as part of your family? How many fingers would you need?*

In our class, are there fewer three- or five-person families? How do you know?	
Marisa	There are fewer families with five people, like mine!
Michael	Yeah, I counted seven families with three people. Seven hands have only three fingers up.
Juliana	There are only three families with five people. I counted the number of hands with five fingers.

MathLand® Smart Strands • Grades K–2
© Creative Publications

4 *Just for fun, let's stand up in our groups to show what the data in the graph would look like.* Help the class organize themselves into clusters based on how many people they have in their families.

5 If you wish, make a bulletin board titled *How Many in Your Family?* Have each child draw a colorful picture of his family. Mount each child's picture on the bulletin board with the cut-out hand that shows the number of people in the family.

The graph the class constructs today is likely to have more than three columns, so it will be more difficult for the children to interpret. Standing up in groups that have the same number of family members may help the children get another perspective on the day's data. For example, it will be easier for the children to see who has the same number in their family as they stand clumped with the people in their group.

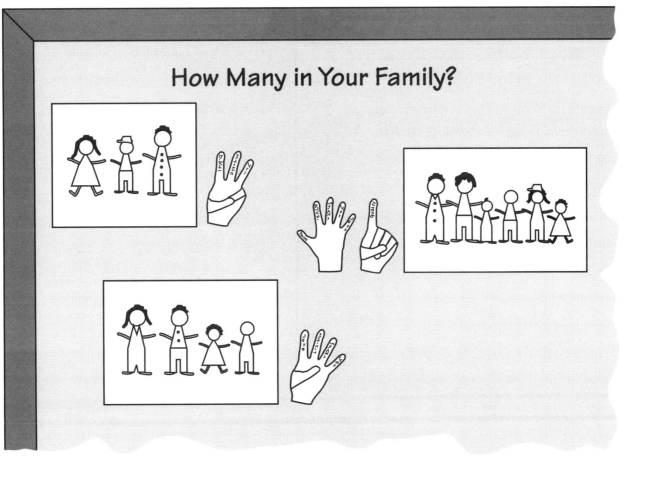

How Many in Your Family?

Graphing Connections

This week, as we make and read bar graphs, we begin to appreciate the organization of information. We learn to make comparisons and see relationships between the information shown by the bars. We ask questions about what information we can tell from the bar graph.

Key Mathematical Ideas

★ Bar graphs are a powerful way to organize and display data.

★ Important comparative information can be drawn from bar graphs.

Prior Knowledge

The children should know how to count to 35. Some experience with pictographs would be helpful. They should know the concepts "more" and "less."

WHAT THE CHILDREN WILL DO

• Collect data and make bar graphs of the data

• Learn to read and draw conclusions from bar graphs

Getting Ready

Materials

• LinkerCubes, 4 per child

• 1-cm grid paper (page 107)

• chart paper

• 3" × 5" index cards, 1 per child

• string

• scissors

Preparation

 • For Day Trip Two, draw a three-column grid with 15 rows on chart paper. The grids should be large enough to contain a shape made with four LinkerCubes. Label each column with one of the three possible shapes. For Day Trip Three, make a transparency of 1-cm grid paper (page 107).

How do we know what our friends like? Today we look at our story preferences. We make a tally chart and then create a bar graph to help us compare the data.

1 *What are some things you and your friends like?* List some of the children's suggestions on the chalkboard. *How do you know they like them? Do you ever change what you like? What makes you change what you like?*

2 *When we ask people what they like, we're collecting data. If we organize that data, we can find out some interesting things.*

3 List the four kinds of stories on the chalkboard. Label them one through four. *Suppose we could choose one kind of story to read to the class. Which kind would we choose?* Pass out index cards and ask the children to write the number of their choice on the card.

4 Have the children come up to the chalkboard and put a tally mark next to their choice. *Now let's show this data another way.* Draw horizontal and vertical axes on chart paper. Label the horizontal axis with the kinds of stories. *Tape your index card on top of the kind of story you chose.*

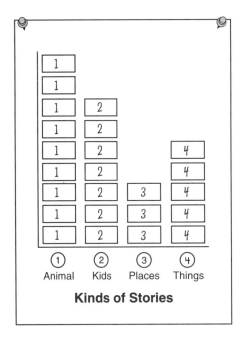

Kinds of Stories

5 Ask children about the graph.

- *Which kind of story did the most people choose? The fewest?*

- *Do you think that this is the class's favorite kind of story? Could there be other favorite types of stories?*

- *Do you think that this kind would be the favorite if we asked more people?*

- *Would a different class vote differently? A different grade? Would adults vote differently?*

- *What else do we know from the graph?*

Bar graphs of preferences don't really tell what people like best. They only tell what people like best among the choices. Through discussion, the children may discover that there are other kinds of stories they like better than those given.

Today we use LinkerCube shapes to make a real object graph that we turn into a bar graph. We see how easy it is to compare data and draw conclusions from the graph.

1 Give each child four LinkerCubes. *Connect the four cubes to make a shape. What different shapes did we make?* Have the children share what they made. Show the class how some shapes may look different, but when turned, they are actually the same.

2 Place the chart you prepared on the floor. *Now place your shape on the graph where it belongs.* On the chalkboard, tally how many children made each shape as they place their shapes on the floor.

3 *Could we represent each shape another way? What if we colored in the square the shape is on? Would that tell us the same information?* Proceed to color in the squares as you take off the shapes. Then post the graph on the wall.

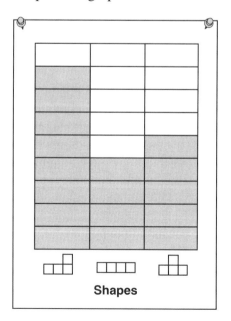

Shapes

4 Discuss the bar graph with the class. Explain that the graph is called a bar graph and that this is another way to represent the data.

- *What do you know from the graph?*

- *Why do you think more people made this shape?*

- *What other questions could we ask?*

- *Do you think another class would have the same results?*

- *Why do you think this is called a bar graph?*

- *What title could we give this graph?*

- *Is it easier to get information by looking at a bar graph or the tallies? Why?*

5 Ask the children to write two things they know from looking at the graph.

It is important for the child to see that the real object graph, the tally chart, and the bar graph all represent the same data. The bar graph, however, makes it easiest to do quick comparisons and to draw conclusions.

MathLand® Smart Strands • Grade K–2
© Creative Publications

Which is worse, a slimy slug or crunchy cockroach? Today we make and read our own bar graphs of yucky things.

1 *Some bugs are cool and some are yucky. Let's make a graph showing which bugs we think are yuckiest. What bugs do you think are yucky?* On the chalkboard, list the children's choices, and then work with the class to combine types of bugs so the graph has three or four choices.

2 With a simple raising of hands, collect the data and make a tally chart. Then on the overhead projector, create a bar graph on transparent 1-cm grid paper.

- *What were our choices?*

- *What should we title our graph?*

- *How many people voted for this choice? How many squares should I color to show that?*

- *How about this choice?*

- *How could we label the graph so we can quickly see how many people voted for this choice?*

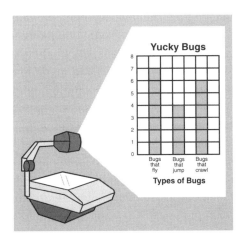

3 Discuss the graph with the class.

- *What do we know from the graph?*

- *What don't we know?*

- *What other graph could we make to find out more?*

4 Pass out 1-cm grid paper to the children. *Now work with a partner to make a graph about things people think are yucky. You and your partner must decide what the graph is about. What sorts of graphs could we make?* On the chalkboard, list the suggestions, such as yuckiest food, worst TV shows, and ickiest chores.

5 *Once you have a topic, think of the choices. Then make a tally sheet to collect your data.* Post the tally sheets and have the children go around and vote. When the class is finished, have the pairs collect their tally sheets and make a bar graph of the data.

6 Have the pairs explain their graphs and what they show. *What is your graph about? What does it show?*

Interview Assessment

As the children create their graphs, ask individuals, *What does the graph show? Does the graph tell us more than a tally sheet does? Does it make a difference what items are used in the graph?*

Are you a square? Today we make a graph that shows what shape we are.

1 *Did you know that some people are tall rectangles, some are wide rectangles, and some are squares?* Draw the three shapes on the chalkboard.

2 *Let's find out what shape we are.* In groups of four, have the children measure each other and write down on scrap paper their shape.

How to Find Out What Shape You Are

Have two friends hold a string taut from your feet to your head and mark your height on the string.

Does your arm span reach from the end of the string to the mark?

If you can reach farther than the mark, you're a wide rectangle.

If you can't reach the mark, you're a long rectangle.

If you can exactly reach the mark, you're a square.

3 On chart paper, have the class tally their results. Then have pairs make a bar graph showing how many children are long rectangles, wide rectangles, and squares.

4 Have a discussion about the graph.

- *What do you know from the graph?*

- *What do you not know?* (whether different classes have different results, whether grown ups are mostly one shape, whether girls are mostly one shape, and so on)

- *Is there anything different between this kind of graph and a graph that asks us to choose which thing we like or dislike?*

As the children work with the shape graph, they will begin to get experience with graphs that portray factual data as opposed to graphs that show preferences. Look to see if they recognize any difference between the kinds of choices.

Home Work

Have pairs pick a topic, either a preference or a fact, and then each child can survey ten people. The children can tally the data and bring it to school so they can use it to make a graph.

Today we use the data we collected for homework to create a bar graph. Then we write about what the graph shows and doesn't show.

1 *Let's make a graph of the data we collected for our homework. What are some of the questions we asked?* Have the children share their survey questions.

2 Pass out 1-cm grid paper to the children and let them begin their graphs.

- *What information do you need to show on your graph?*

- *What are the different choices? Where will you label them on your graph?*

- *How will you know how many squares to fill in?*

- *How will you tell people what your graph is about?*

- *What will you do to make sure someone else can read your graph?*

3 When the class is finished, ask the children to write two things they know from their bar graph and one thing that their bar graph doesn't tell them for sure. Ask them to describe what other graph they could make to find out more.

4 Place the graphs on the wall and choose a few to talk about. There are likely to be several bar graphs on similar topics. Ask the children to compare the information in those graphs. Look for conclusions that relate to more than one bar graph.

Math Journal

Ask the children to write how their graphs might change if they surveyed more people.

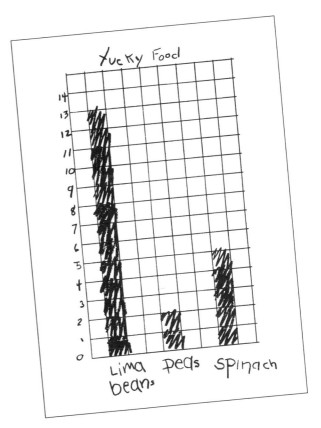

Hot and Cold

This week we'll work with temperature in several ways. We'll categorize objects and events related to hot and cold temperatures. We'll learn to read temperatures using a thermometer. We'll also study the differences in temperature around the United States.

Key Mathematical Ideas

★ Weather and temperature present many mathematical situations.

★ Thermometers measure temperature in Celsius scale and Fahrenheit scale.

★ Temperatures vary around the United States.

Prior Knowledge

Children should have experience constructing and interpreting graphs. They should also be able to skip count by two, up to 100.

WHAT THE CHILDREN WILL DO

- *Categorize objects by function*

- *Read temperatures on a thermometer in both Fahrenheit and Celsius degrees*

- *Record temperature changes on a thermometer*

- *Collect and read data related to temperature*

Getting Ready

Materials

- Student thermometers

- Magazines

- Weather pages from local newspapers

- Fabric scraps

- Scissors

- Glue

Preparation

• For Day Trip One, gather items that are used in cold weather, hot weather, or both (see page 89 for suggestions), and set out 3 large boxes. For Day Trip Two, prepare fabric scraps and "Weather Reports" (see page 90) and make copies of the Dress Me Up (page 104) for each pair. For Day Trips Three, Four, and Five, make several copies of Reading a Thermometer (page 105) for each child.

Today we'll think of what we need for real-world weather conditions. We'll connect these objects to what we know about hot and cold temperatures.

1 Display your collection of items that are used for particular weather conditions. Use the following suggestions:

Items for hot weather	Items for cold weather
beach ball	mittens or gloves
sunscreen	scarf
shorts	sweater
sandals	wool hat
T-shirt	boots

Items for both
sunglasses
umbrella

2 Label a box "Hot Weather," another box "Cold Weather," and a third box "Both Hot and Cold." *I am organizing my closets, and I want to separate these items into what I need for hot or cold weather.* Have one child at a time choose an item and put it in the appropriate box. Discuss why a certain box was used for each object.

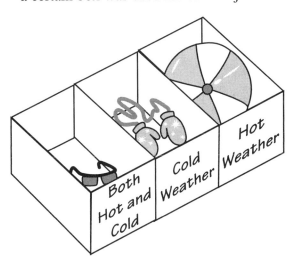

3 Construct a large classroom graph with category headings: Hot Weather, Cold Weather, Both Hot and Cold. Give each pair an old magazine. *Find some pictures that show hot and cold weather activities.* Have the children suggest a few pictures for each category. After children cut out several examples, have them tape the pictures on the chart under the appropriate category.

4 Discuss the children's findings. *Did we find more examples of things that show cold weather or hot weather? What kinds of things did we find that showed both hot and cold?*

Home Work Have children prepare a recording sheet with Hot Foods, Cold Foods, and Warm Foods. Then they write a list or draw their favorite foods under each category. Compare the lists in class.

Today we'll be deciding on what clothes we need to wear for different climates. Then we'll make an outfit to match the weather.

1 *Let's look at what type of clothing we are wearing.* Discuss what made children decide to wear long pants instead of shorts, short sleeves instead of a sweater, and so on. *We often need to know the weather before getting dressed each day. What are some ways we can find out what the weather is like outside?*

2 *What kind of clothing do we need to protect ourselves outside on a cold day? What should we wear to be comfortable on a hot day? on a rainy day?* Divide the class into pairs. Write a few descriptive words on pieces of paper and give one "Weather Report" to each pair. Add pictures for the younger children, such as a sun, cloud with raindrops, or a snowman.

3 Distribute a copy of Dress Me Up. *Read your "Weather Report." Think about what would be good to wear. Look through the fabric scraps and pick out materials that those clothes might be made of. Make an outfit that will protect you in that weather.* Provide glue and scissors. Cutting fabric will be difficult, so remind children that clothes don't need to be shaped perfectly.

4 Have pairs read their weather report and describe the outfit they created. *What would the outdoor temperature be like if you wore your outfit? Could you wear the outfit if the temperature was cold? Could you wear the outfit if the temperature was warm?*

Math Journal

What is the temperature like during your favorite season? In your journal, draw a picture and write about your favorite season of the year.

Today we'll learn to read a thermometer that shows the temperature in Celsius scale and in Fahrenheit scale.

1 Hold up a thermometer. ***What is this called? What is it used for? Where have you seen thermometers before?*** Remind the class that thermometers are fragile and must be handled with care. Distribute Student Thermometers, one to each pair.

> A thermometer is a small glass tube partially filled with liquid. When the temperature gets warmer, the liquid expands. This causes it to rise in the tube. The warmer the temperature, the higher the liquid rises.

2 ***Look at the top of the thermometer. Find the letters F and C. The left side of the thermometer shows the Fahrenheit scale. The right side of the thermometer shows the Celsius scale. Let's read aloud the numbers on the Fahrenheit side. Now let's read aloud the numbers on the Celsius side. What can you tell about the numbers?*** *The United States uses Fahrenheit to measure temperature. Most scientists and other countries use Celsius to measure temperature.*

> Have children compare the lines on the thermometer to the lines on a number line. Refer to the number line in your classroom or draw a short number line on the chalkboard. For children who need practice, begin at zero on the Fahrenheit side and count the degrees by twos together as a group. Then count the degrees on the Celsius side.

3 ***We use the word*** **degrees** ***when we work with temperatures. Each line in the thermometer stands for 2 degrees. Let's measure the temperature of the room. What number on the Fahrenheit side is closest to the top of the red line? What number on the Celsius side is closest to the top of the red line?***

4 Use a large demonstration thermometer or draw a thermometer on the chalkboard. Move the gauge up and down and have children read different temperatures in Celsius and Fahrenheit. Demonstrate how to write the temperature, for example, 70° F.

5 Reading a Thermometer (page 105), can be used in a variety of ways. Choose one or more of the following activities:

• Dictate a temperature. Children write the temperature next to the thermometer. Then they draw a red line on the thermometer that shows the temperature.

• Write temperatures next to the thermometers before copying. Children draw a red line that shows the temperature. Cut apart the squares and order the thermometers from lowest to highest temperature.

• Draw the lines on the thermometers before copying. Have children read the thermometer and write the correct temperature.

• Write a time of day at the top of each thermometer. Have the children read an outdoor thermometer and mark their worksheets throughout the day.

Today we'll experiment with changing temperatures and practice reading thermometers.

1 Distribute thermometers, one per pair. *What is the temperature of our room? Without going outside, can you think of a way to make the thermometer show a lower temperature? How can you make it show a higher temperature?*

2 Children may try taking measurements near a sunny window, on a tile floor, near a fluorescent light, and inside their desks. You may want to have cups filled with cool water, soil, and other substances available for them to measure with their thermometers. (Do set up some guidelines. Children should not place the thermometer directly on a heater or in hot water. They also shouldn't use appliances to increase the temperature.)

3 Hand out copies of Reading a Thermometer (page 105). *Use a red crayon to draw the temperature on a thermometer, then write the area where you recorded it.* Have pairs take turns experimenting with changing the temperature on the thermometers.

Robbie	Near the window the thermometer changed to 75 degrees.
Juliana	Inside my desk it's only 68 degrees.

4 If children haven't thought of it, have them use their bodies to show an increase of temperature on the thermometer. *Hold the bulb of the thermometer with your thumb and finger. How high does the temperature go? Hold the thermometer between your neck and your shoulder. How high is the temperature there?*

5 *What was the highest temperature you recorded? Where was it? Where was the lowest temperature you recorded?* Record the data on a chart. Older children can figure out the difference between the highest and lowest temperatures.

WHAT'S THE TEMPERATURE?	
Place	Temperature
By window	70° F
By lights	80° F
By door	68° F
By heater	76° F
In closet	71° F
In desk	69° F

6 If weather permits, continue the experiment outdoors. *Where might you find the highest temperature? Where might you find the lowest temperature?*

Interview Assessment	As the children work, approach individuals and ask them to read a temperature they have recorded on their worksheet.

Today we'll study the weather across the country. We'll use newspaper weather maps to compare the highest and lowest temperatures.

1 *There are many ways to learn about the weather. Today we are going to look at temperatures around the United States, using a weather map from a newspaper.* Distribute several copies of today's weather page. (Use a colored weather map if possible.) *How can we tell where it is cold? How can we tell where it is warm?*

2 *Many maps will use colors to show the temperatures in different areas of the country. Other maps will record the temperature directly on the map. Let's find our state. What temperature does the map show?* Distribute copies of Read a Thermometer, page 105. *Draw the temperature on a thermometer. Write "Our State" and the date next to the thermometer. Let's find the temperature for some other states. Record the temperatures on the worksheet.*

3 *If there is a detailed map of the local weather, ask children to find the high and low temperatures for your town or city. What will our weather be like tomorrow? Look at the weather predictions for the week. How do you think a weatherperson predicts the weather? Why is it important to be able to predict the weather?*

TODAY	TOMORROW	SATURDAY	SUNDAY
Mostly cloudy, a few sprinkles likely. Highs, 51-58. Lows, 40-50.	Partly cloudy with showers by evening. Highs, 55-60. Lows, 43-52.	Partly cloudy after a morning shower. Highs, 55-60. Lows, 38-46.	Mostly sunny with mild conditions. Highs, 57-62. Lows, 37-45.

Review other details of the weather page as appropriate for your class. International temperatures, rainfall and snow levels, high and low tides, and so on provide a wealth of measurement possibilities.

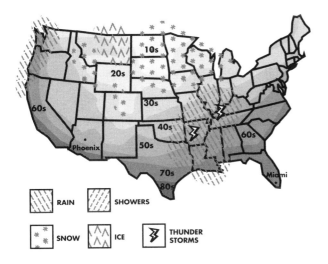

Scarecrows

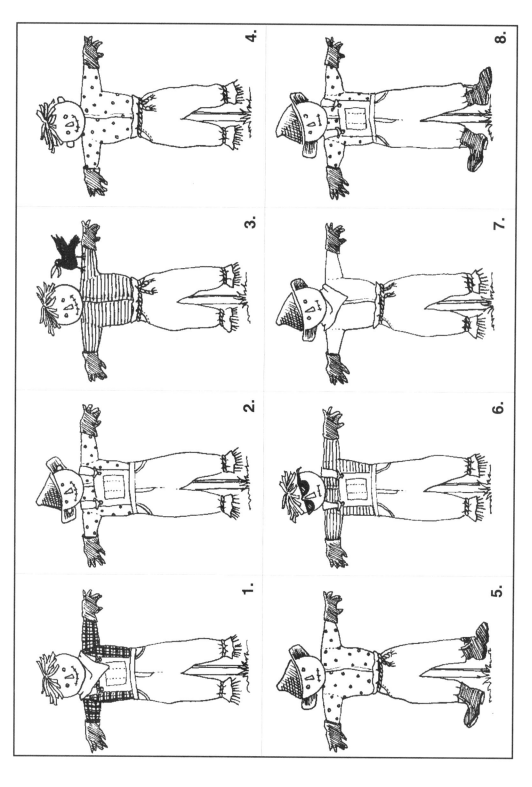

MathLand® Smart Strands • Grades K–2
© Creative Publications

Harvest Time

Which is more? $\frac{1}{4}$ of 20 apples $\frac{1}{5}$ of 15 apples	Which is more? $\frac{1}{6}$ of 18 potatoes $\frac{1}{5}$ of 20 potatoes
Which is more? $\frac{2}{3}$ of 9 beets $\frac{2}{5}$ of 10 beets	Which is more? $\frac{3}{4}$ of 16 carrots $\frac{2}{3}$ of 15 carrots
Which is more? $\frac{3}{8}$ of 24 pears $\frac{1}{3}$ of 24 pears	Which is more? $\frac{3}{6}$ of 24 peas $\frac{3}{4}$ of 20 peas

Number Line

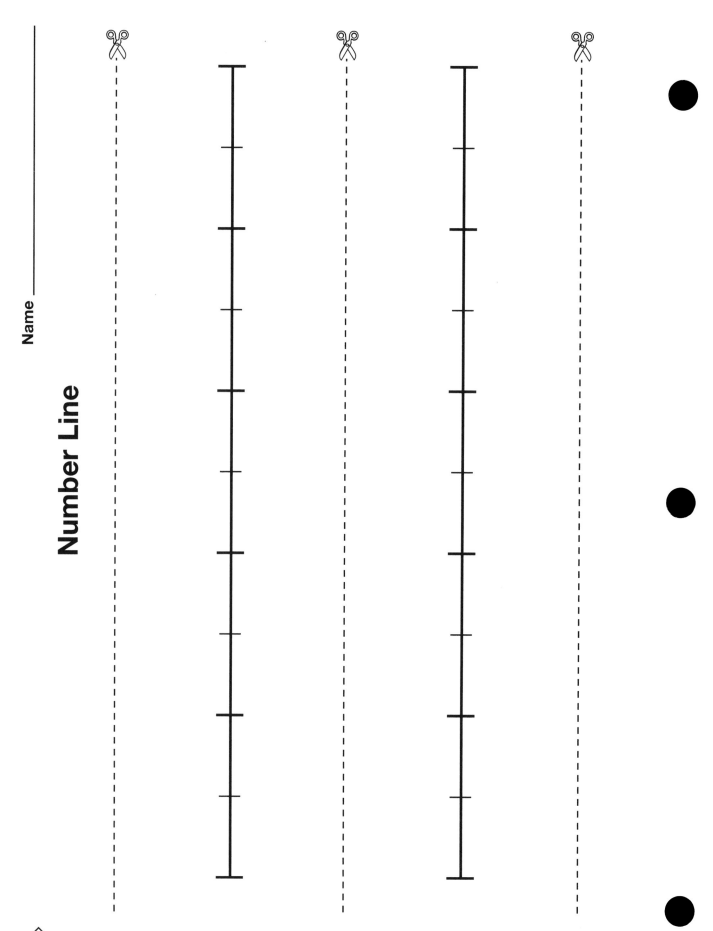

MathLand® Smart Strands • Grades K–2
© Creative Publications

Matching Shapes

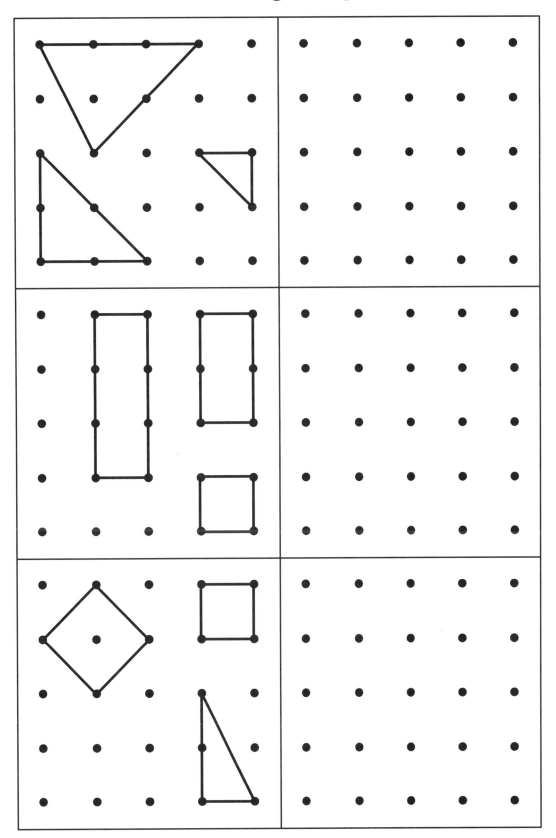

MathLand® Smart Strands • Grades K–2
© Creative Publications

Note to the Teacher:
Permission is given to reproduce this page.

97

2-cm Dot Paper

MathLand® Smart Strands • Grades K–2
© Creative Publications

Measurement Hunt

Find things that are about:

MathLand® Smart Strands • Grades K–2
© Creative Publications

Note to the Teacher:
Permission is given to reproduce this page.

99

How Many Cups?

Container	Estimate	Actual
Half-Pint		
Pint		
Quart		
Half-Gallon		
Gallon		
Liter		

MathLand® Smart Strands • Grades K–2
© Creative Publications

Mayan Calendar Symbols

The Mayan calendar consisted of 18 months–each with 20 days
plus an additional period of 5 days, totaling 365.

Mayan Months

Mayan Days

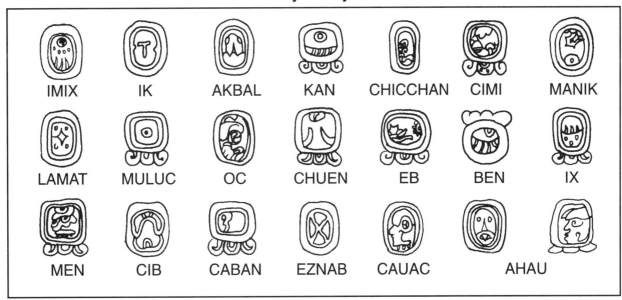

MathLand® Smart Strands • Grades K–2
© Creative Publications

Note to the Teacher:
Permission is given to reproduce this page.

101

Bike Orders

4 bikes

5 bikes

6 bikes

7 bikes

8 bikes

9 bikes

10 bikes

_____ **bikes**

MathLand® Smart Strands • Grades K–2

Name _____

Out | **In**

Rule _____

Out | **In**

Rule _____

Out | **In**

Rule _____

Out | **In**

Rule _____

Out | **In**

Rule _____

Out | **In**

Rule _____

Number Machine

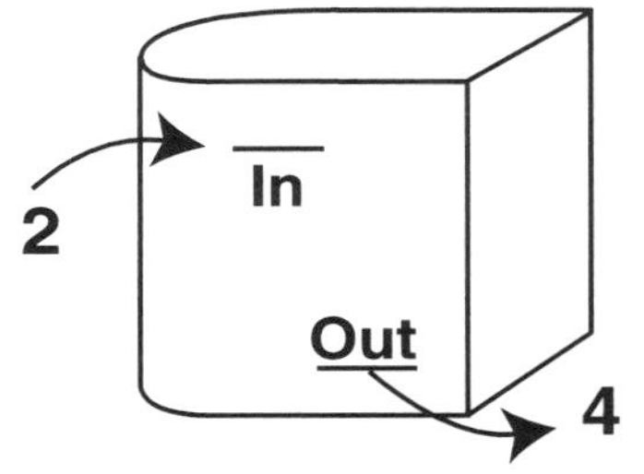

In

Out

2

4

MathLand® Smart Strands • Grades K–2
© Creative Publications

Note to the Teacher:
Permission is given to reproduce this page.

103

Dress Me Up

MathLand® Smart Strands • Grades K–2
© Creative Publications

Reading a Thermometer

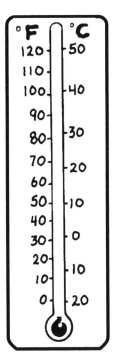

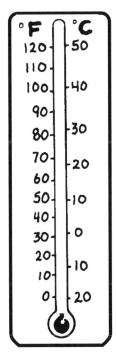

MathLand® Smart Strands • Grades K–2
© Creative Publications

Note to the Teacher:
Permission is given to reproduce this page.

105

1-inch Grid

MathLand® Smart Strands • Grades K–2
© Creative Publications

Name _____

1-cm Grid

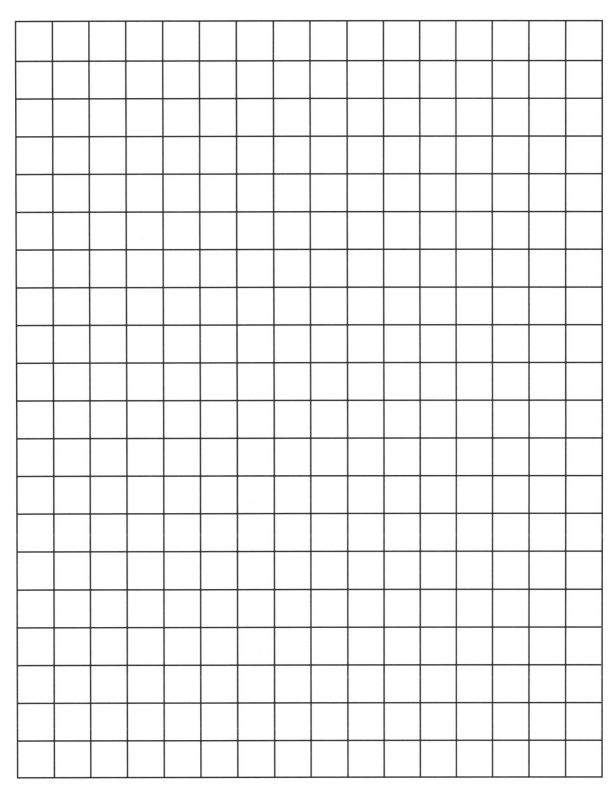

Geoboard Dot Paper

MathLand® Smart Strands • Grades K–2